DAY TRADING STRATEGIES

2 books in 1: Master the best methods to sistematically generate passive income. Learn how to trade for a living as a pro and get positive ROI in 7 days with options and forex

MARK BROKER

TABLE OF CONTENTS

INTRODUCTION

I In this book, we will talk about two types of trading: day trading and swing trading. On this extended version we added a part about Options Trading. It is necessary for every beginner to understand all the sections. In order to start your career as a successful trader, you should have some basic knowledge about trading. This book will help you to clarify your doubts regarding day, swing and options trading, how they should invest their money and which trade will give them more profit.

Day trading is defined as the activity of capturing profit from the variation of stock prices during the day. In other words, day trading is about selling and buying stocks in a short time.

On the other side, swing trading is defined as the activity of buying and selling stocks during a time span of more than one day.

"Trading" is intended as the set of actions aimed to making extra-income money through investment strategies. Those who apply trading strategy in the financial market for gaining profit and helding a position in the market are known as "Swing Traders." Swing traders typically focus on getting profit by small gains in a very short time span. Their position in the market may be held for several days or for a week. They buy some stocks on the market and then sell them when they believe they can get a good profit on it. It is a process going on between a buyer and a seller. Swing traders keep their check and balance in the market; then, with the help of technical analysis, they identify the price swings and determine whether buy a stock or not, whether prices are rising, or they can come out with a loss. Swing traders risk 0.5% on each trade; nevertheless they pursue much higher goals in terms of profit by each trade. Most of the traders buy the stock when they prices are low and sell them when the prices are higher in the market. In some cases, this strategy causes losses, because the stock values decrease (this happens in very rare cases, though).

Most people make confusion between swing trading with day trading. In reality, swing trading is far different from day trading because day trading has lower chances of getting losses than swing trading. Also, in day trading, the time of trading is limited (one day), whereas in swing trading there is no time limit: it is indeed an overnight process. The market of swing traders works for 24hours; therefore, the profit/loss chances are higher because the seller can face the downfall anytime. Swing traders are also rewarded by a leverage of 50%. For example, if a trader is allowed to have a margin in his trading, then he only needs to invest $20,000 for a trade rather than investing $40,000. It is a process through which it is possible to helding profit for a long time. This process is not about getting profit in a day, but it could go from a day to many days. There will be more chances of getting profit than loss. For beginners, swing trading is the best option to choose because swing trading is easy and there are more chances of succeed with it. It is, in fact, less stressful for a seller and it is associated to higher success probability with respect to day trading, since time allows to improve accuracy in investment decision. It is well known that swing traders have several opportunities and options to trade. They may get more opportunities to invest their money during the longer investment time-span. It is very important for a trader be concerned in the price variation of their stock and be patient. After all, everything is all about profit and loss.

So far, all the websites or books about day and swing trading that I have been reading were unfit to a clear understanding of how to enter or exit in any trading system. I wrote this book so that it will help the coming generations to understand what day and swing trading are about, and investing their money on the type of trading that suits better to them.

The options are a particular type of derivative instrument that gives the possibility to buy or sell at a set price, a specific underlying asset, which represents the object of the option contract.

The term "option" comes from the word possibility. The options offer the opportunity to buy or sell an asset. It therefore represents a right for the subscriber and not an obligation.

The terms call, put, strike price, at the money and in the money are all connected to the option management operations. Their meaning, as we will see, is much more intuitive and immediate than it might seem.

The recent evolution of financial markets have given great prominence to options and their particular variations such as binary options. They are considered as profitable and versatile financial instruments to trading strategies. They will offer many savers the opportunity to build pay-off portfolios through the aggregation of different tools.

1. DIFFERENCE BETWEEN SWING TRADING AND DAY TRADING

If you are a beginner, then keep your mind open for both types of trading, do not waste your money or time in investing until you do not have enough knowledge about the trading systems. For a beginner, there is always a lot of things to learn about, whatever the field is learning about your interest is very important. Before starting any trading pattern, it is necessary to understand your needs and expectations that you have related to the trading system. First of all, the trader who wants to trade should know how much active trading he wants. Whether he wants a trading system that survives in the market for a longer time, or not. What are his current requirements and expectations related to trading whether he can handle his trading system for a long time, or did he have enough stamina to bear the loss? Once you decide the right path that suits you and that you believe can fulfill your expectation, then you can easily survive in the trading market.

Traders have divided trading into two parts swing trading and day trading. This book will help you to understand the difference between both the trading systems, and it will help you in choosing which trading system is best for you. The main goal of any beginner is to gain profit on their stock, whether it's a day trader or a swing trader; at the end of the day, every trader needs their name in a profit list. Even though both tradings has different tools and technical analysis procedures.

Day trading is about making multiples trades in a day. As the name suggests doing trade on your stock within a day but multiple times is day trading. This trade is all about doing trade within a day or hours. You cannot go beyond that time, and it doesn't matter how many times you trade in a day. The main objective of the day traders is to make money from their preexisting income in a day with their stock. This trade is only about day trading; it does not contain night hours. They do not keep any overnight securities. The biggest advantage of day trading is that the trader has fewer chances of having any kind of loss. For example, if a trader invests their money on any stock and the market rate of that stock goes down in the middle of the night, so in that case, the trader has to face a loss, but because of day trading, the chances of losses are also less as they will not invest their money for overnight.

According to the U.S Securities and Exchange Commission (SEC), "The Day traders typically suffer financial losses in their first months of trading, and many never graduate to profit-making status." After the SEC cautions the day trader, it was easy to understand that the beginner's traders should not take a risk by investing money more than they can afford, they should not go beyond their limitations. Most of the people commit suicide when they face loss because they had borrowed money from their friends and family or from other sources.

The day traders do not need any partner, they usually work alone, and they do not have their flexible schedule, and they do their work according to their mood and needs. They usually work at their places and take off and rap all of their stuff whenever they want. They do not need anyone's instruction because they do their work independently.

Sometimes it becomes difficult for the beginners of day traders to compete in the market because except making money and position in the market they also have to compete with the high-frequency traders, whereas other faces more advantages than the beginners as they become professionals in their work and have more experience than them. Once you start getting profit on your stock, there will be no come back from this earning adventure; you will desire to invest more and earn more.

The day trader has to generate a lot of effort and use his skills to maintain the position in the market. A beginner who wants to have all the luxuries firstly had to quit his job to maintain all his focus on trading because it would not be easy for a day trader to continue his job as it all depends on you to keep check and balance in the market. Because day trading is stressful, and the trader has to keep his self-up-to date with the ongoing situation in the market. He should be aware of multiple screening so it will help him to spot the trading opportunities.

For example

If someone is continuous his job with day trading and on the opposite hand the shares of an organization like Walmart (WMT) or Apple (AAPL) within the forex market are going high, and there's an excellent opportunity for him to trade his currency like euro or U.S. dollar (EUR/USD), so he will miss the prospect due to his job routine.

So it will be better for the future of the trader to just focus on one thing at a time, his job or a business. For trading, there are various markets; the ups and downs in the market make easier for those who cannot afford it. Once the stocks go down, buyers borrow them and sell them when the rate goes high. In the forex market, it is easier for beginners to invest their money as it requires the least capital for trading purposes. You can start from a little amount like $50, but if you can invest a large amount so it will be more useful. To gain a good position in the market, stocks trade requires to be at least $25,000 to make day trade. Day trade stock requires more capital for the better position, but if you do not have $25,000 or can't maintain your account above $25,000 then stocks are not the right place for you to invest money or do not waste your time on it, but if you have crossed $25,000, then stocks are viable day trading market. Long-time day traders love the joys of pitting their wits against the market and other professionals day in and time out. The adrenaline rush from rapid-fire trading are a few things not many traders will admit to, but it's a giant think about their decision to create a living from day trading. It's doubtful these styles of people would be content spending their days selling widgets or perusing numbers in an office cubicle.

Day trading and swing trading each have advantages and downsides. Neither strategy is healthier than the opposite, and traders should choose the approach that works best for his or her skills, preferences, and lifestyle. Day trading is healthier suited to individuals who are smitten by trading full time and possess the three Ds: decisiveness, discipline, and diligence (prerequisites for successful day trading). Swing trading, on the opposite hand, doesn't require such a formidable set of traits. Since swing trading will be undertaken by anyone with some investment capital and doesn't require full-time attention, it's a viable option for traders who want to stay their full-time jobs, but also dabble within the markets. Swing traders should even be able to apply a mixture of fundamental and technical analysis, instead of technical analysis alone.

If we differentiate swing and day trading, then they both are far different from each other, their framing time to trade is different. Swing trading is about selling and buying stock for days and weeks. Swing traders have more time to trade then the day traders. Their trading frame is longer than then day traders as they hold a position overnight. Because of their 24 hours of trading, they cannot avoid the risk that can cause a big problem against them. There will be more chances of losing money in this trade. They have to worry about the stock all the time because it could be different while opening, or it could be different from how it closed before the day. Swing traders need a lot of patience because he had to face many problems. Trades generally need time to figure out. Keeping a trade for an asset open for some days or weeks may lead to higher profits than trading in and out of the identical security multiple times daily. Swing traders know that it will take a long time, but they generally do not make it look like a full-time job. Swing trade may take a few days or maybe a few weeks to work out. Swing traders do not make this trading a full-time job career like day traders. If you have enough knowledge about swing trading and investment capital that you can try swing trading. If you are a beginner in trading and want to invest your money, then swing trading is a perfect choice because it does not require your 24/7 hours' attention, or you do not need to glued yourselves in front of your computers and keeping your eyes and fingers crossed all the time. A swing trader can even do a full-time job if he wants to because swing trading doesn't require checking on the screens all the time. The margin requirements in swing trading are higher, and usually, its maximum leverage is two times one's capital, whereas day trading has four times and one's capitals. It doesn't need constant monitoring like day trading; it can be stopped anytime whenever you feel like there is a risk in executing the trading process.

Like any other trading swing trading can also result in substantial losses. Infect swing traders has to face a larger loss than day traders as swing traders hold their position in the market for a longer time. That's why they run the risk of larger loss than day trading. Swing traders usually do have their regular jobs, and they also have other sources of income from where they can overcome theirs loses. There are more chances of burnout for swing traders due to stress in swing trading since it's seldom a full-time job. Swing traders have more chances through which they can mitigate or offset their losses.

Swing trading can be done by having just one computer, and with conventional trading tools unlike, day trading it does not require the art technology. Swing traders have overnight leverage of 50% as compared to day trading, but this margin can be risky too, particularly if margin calls occur. These trading are not so much about what you want to trade, be it commodities, i.e., oil futures or stock from the CAC 40. Instead of that, it is simply all about timing. So, where it took 4 hours and daily charts of day trading, it will be more concerned about swing trading where it took multi-day charts and candlestick patterns. Moving average crossovers, Head and shoulders patterns, shooting stars, etc. are some of the most popular.

Swing trading can be extremely challenging in two markets, the bear market environment or raging bull market. Here you will see even highly active traders will not display in the same position there will be same up and down oscillation. To invest in the stock market, it's compulsory to have a well-organized method for trading. It is very important to keep things simple, as in the early stages, it will look a bit difficult for the beginners, but instead of getting panic, they should handle them with confidence. Once you learn the rules of swing trading and the discipline, you will make money in a great quantity in the stock market. Swing trading allows you to trade in every situation, whether it is bullish, bearish, or just going sideways. This is another reason why this trade has a distinct advantage over other approaches to invest in a swing trade.

Swing traders use technical analysis indicators to identify the price swings in the market and determine the condition of the market, whether a stock price will drop or rise in the short run. Through this, they invest the capitalize in securities that have momentum and select the best time for buying or selling the stock. These technical analysis indicators help the traders to use the swing charts for their swing trading on the security current situation trend. To analyze the current trading pattern, swing traders use swing trading charts, which help the trader in providing data based on statistical analysis. Unlike day trading, swing trading is not about the long term value of the security; instead of that, they are just concerned about the ups and downs in the stock price. Swing traders can make large returns on the stock that decay in value over time because they are making returns on each small price swing of their stock while the overall trend is downward.

Swing trading and day trading appears similar in some aspects of trading. The main factor of trading is setting the two techniques apart and maintaining the position on time in the market. Unlike day traders, it does not close within minutes or in hours, it takes several weeks and overnight days. They are subjected to the unpredictability of overnight risks that may result in significant price momentum. Swing traders can check their positions in the market periodically and can take action when critical points are reached.

Main differences between swing trading and day trading are:

Trading times:

Both of them have different timings of trading. In day trading, it takes a maximum of two to four hours daily for trading purposes, and in this time, the trader manages to analyze the charts, entering and getting out of the positions, and review different stocks. Whereas the swing trader's minimum needs 45 minutes in a day, update his order and find the new one. Day trading demands more time than swing trading.

Risks:

Day trader experiences more losses than swing traders because day traders may need to carry out six trades per day, whereas swing traders may need to carry out six trades per month to maintain a good position in the market. That's why day traders had to face more struggle in maintaining their position in the market as their risk level is higher than swing traders, and they had to engage their selves more in the market then swing traders.

Stress:

Day traders are more in stress as they have to keep their selves engage all the time with the market situation. They need great knowledge about market movements and had a great level of patience. A day trader needs to be more focused on their work. On the other hand, swing traders do not take that much pressure and can't say that they are much focused than day traders.

2. HOW DOES IT WORK?

What is swing trading?

"Swing trading is a technique used for buying and selling stocks."

How does it work?

Swing trading is one of the most used and common trading strategies used in almost every market, including forex, futures trading, stocks, and much more. Swing trading is about buying and selling the stock, buying it from the market, and selling it for gains. For this purpose, traders mostly rely on technical analysis to spot good selling and buying opportunities.

Subsequently, swing trading mostly relays on fundamental assets since its great determent of significant price movements. Sometimes it will take days and even weeks. It also helps to improve trade analysis. Therefore, a trader can verify where the fundamental assets are favorable or not, or it could potentially improve instead of relying on the bearish patterns. Swing traders use the technical analysis indicator to identify the price of swing trade and determine whether a stock price will rise in the market or drop. By experiencing technical indicators, swing traders are not concerned about the long term value of the stock.

How to make swing trade with trends?

Swing trading is one of the best solid tradings, and it has one of the obvious trends in trading strategies. For beginners, it is necessary to understand its importance in the market that once you get to know how to invest your money, it will offer a lot of high possibility of trading opportunities with a high upside. For a beginner, it is obligatory to have enough knowledge about the market. The initial step that every beginner should take is to identify the market needs, he should know about the market trends.

For getting a good position in the market, every trader should go with the best trends, any trend that goes on the top of the list that if you show them to a child, they would clearly choose the right one whose prices are getting higher or lower.

Price making move lower

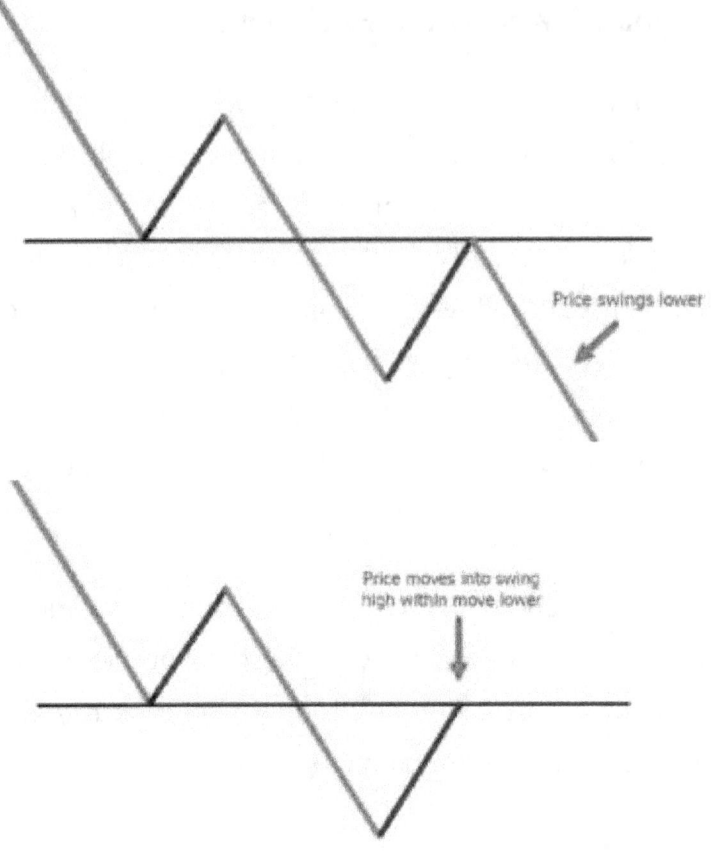

One of the most common mistakes that every beginner makes when looking to swing trade within a trend is not entering with the right swing point.

Tips for Beginners

When you should choose Swing trading:

Swing trading is easier than day trading, but to see whether choosing swing trading is a good decision for you or not, you should enlist all the points and see which one will give you more profit.

- Make sure that you are ready to spend your days, weeks, and months on this trading as swing trading contains a longer period for trading.

- If you already have a job and want to invest your money for extra income, but you do not have enough time to sit in front of a computer, then swing trading is the best option for you.

- You do not need to do constant monitoring and keeping an eye on market activities.

- Swing trading will give you a less stressful life and will reduce the risk level.

- As a beginner, you should always have a plan and stick to it as it's the nature of buying and selling that there will be highs and lows, but you should stick to the plan.

- Before you start swing trading, you should practice it by watching markets. Having knowledge about pre-trading will help you in gaining the loss.

- Don't expect to have money on a quick note; just focus on your aim and let the process sink in.

- Having a good observation will help you in investing money in the right stock, so if you want to gain money on the first stock, then you should know how to use the technical analysis indicators.

- It is important for a beginner to keep in mind while trading the entrance and exit strategy. Before entering a market, we should check everything and keep ourselves update with the study of the charts, noting the price the stock will likely reach in its current swing.

- Most of the traders (like partygoers) find it more favorable to choose how to exit before they have entered the trade.

- There will be more chances of losing money in the earlier stages of trading, but a good trader should stick to it and should gather basic skills, polish those skills, learn new technical techniques, and improve your knowledge. It's important not to give up in a condition.

- He should read books and follow the swing trading tips for beginners.

Trading Platforms

For successful swing trading, the trader should select the right stocks to make a profit in the market. Therefore, traders can also opt for stock with large market capitalization. The most active assets will be among beginners, and they will be the most actively traded ones on top exchange. If we talk about the platforms for swing trading, then, on the one hand, there is a bear market, and on the other is the bull market. Similarly, there is a stable market between both of them. Yet swing trading in a bear or bull market is pretty different from that stable one.

For example, stocks in the market might tend to spike and dump using various patterns in both of these markets, unlike a stable market where a similar pattern could have upheld for weeks or months. In the bear market and bull market, the momentum can cause stocks to trade in a specific way for a long time. In that situation, to gain the maximum profit, a trader should trade in the way of the long term trend. And to experience that profit, a swing trader has to correctly regulate the current market, whether it is bearish or bullish.

The simple moving average (SMA) recommends specific support and resistance stages. It also displays bullish and bearish patterns. When the stock knockouts the support level, it signals a virtuous time to purchase, and once it hits the resistance level, then it's a good time to trade. The bullish and bearish methods also signal entry and exit price points. Therefore, another form of SMA is the exponential moving average (EMA), and it focuses on state-of-the-art data points. The trend signals, as well as entry or exit points presented by the EMA, is quicker compared to the SMA. The 9, 13, and 50 periods EMA can be used to improved time entry points.

For example, when the price of a stock crosses these EMAs, it shows a bullish trend. Therefore, there could probably be a problem with the bearish trend. For instance, when the 9 EMA crosses the 13 EMA, whereas the 13 EMA is above the 50-period EMA, it signals a buying opportunity.

What is day trading?

"Selling and buying a stock multi times in a day."

How does day trading work?

It seems very interesting to trade, and those who wanted to join this trading system may see it with more interest because it seems very easy and interesting, but in reality, the life of a trader is like living a life on the edge. In day trading, we don't have any idea what will happen in the very next moment; unexpected event scan occur at any time. The bitter reality of trading is that most of the days are dry and are quite ordinary, and at the very next moment, you will see your name at the top of the list. In day trading, the high speed of execution is very important as you may see the high numbers of trades you could make in a day to match yourself with the market price you need to match the level of the market. To make your trading work, it is very important to lower the commission rates. It will be more viable day trading as it will have a lower fee rate. Beginners should keep regulatory compliance in their trading. Day traders usually start off with zero positions in their typical portfolios, and day traders trade so frequently that by the end of the day, they have closed all of their trades.

Some day traders work manually, making trade by trade hour by the hour using a chart. Others set up an automatic process that makes orders to purchase and trade for them. Whereas day traders don't actually look at fundamental data, they are concerned in price volatility, liquidity, breaking trends, and trading volume of the day that will change a stock price significantly.

REMINDER:

For day trading, forex is the best platform. For practicing forex and futures trading, a trader should use the Ninja Trader Replay feature. It will help in practicing historical trade days as if you are trading for real.

How to make day trade with trends?

It's very necessary for a trader to follow the market trends for getting a strong position in a market. Trading against the trend and not following it is one of the most common reasons for facing failure in trading. Poor quality of trend and not following a trend is a major reason for not getting the buyer's attention. Those who follow quality and strong trends have more chances of gaining success in trading. In trading, the trend raises the over-all direction of a stock's price. There is another possibility of having traders who are not mentally and physically active all the time to respond to a large number of stocks or price changes. For those who cannot manage things by themselves, they can use a stock screener; it will help the trader to narrow down the number of stocks and decrease the size so that it will make things easier in working for you. If you follow the trending tactics, only trade stocks that have a trending tendency. If you have a stock screener or an assistant, then they can help you isolating stocks that trend so that you will be having a list of stocks, and you can easily apply your day trading strategies through it. Whatever stock you choose to trade represents your trading style, and a good trading style always held a good position in the market.

For stocks, the finest time for day trading is the first one to two hours after the opening, and the last hour before the closing of the market. 9:30 a.m. to 11:30 a.m. The chances of good day trading opportunities usually start a bit earlier than others in the stock market. The forex market trades 24-hours a day throughout the week. The EURUSD is the famous day trading pair. This currency pair usually records better trading volumes between 1

A.M. and 12 P.M. EST. London markets are opened during these hours. Day traders would trade within these hours. The hours from 7 A.M. to 10 A.M. EST typically generate the biggest price changes because both the London and New York markets are opened during this duration. Therefore, this is a very common and active time for day traders.

Tips for Beginners

When you should choose day trading:

For a beginner, it is very important to make a list of all those things that can help him in becoming a good trader and list all those negative points too that can create a problem. Choosing the correct time for trading is very important when you are mentally and physically ready to devote yourself to this path.

- Firstly, see whether you are fulfilling all the requirements of SEC and FINRA pattern day trader rule.

- Give yourself a minute and think that whether you are ready to sit in front of a computer for two to four hours continuously for keeping yourself update from the current situation of the market.

- You need a lot of patience to become a good trader; that's why it is very important to keep your patience level up.

- A trader does not need a college degree or professional degree for day trading. Neither a trader needs to learn thousands of books.

- Discipline is very important for trading; if you start violating everything, then you can never trade your stock in the market.

- A day trader should have the ability to take a risk and managing things if he faces the loss.

- He should not take stress over things but should control them in a good manner.

- You should have a computer for trading, having two monitors is preferable but not necessary. Your computer should have a great memory and fast processer as it can give you a disadvantage if the processer or software is not good.

- Having a good internet connection is another most important thing if you lose the connection during a trade than you will also lose the trade too.

- To start your trading career, it is necessary to select the right platform. As the beginners do not have enough knowledge about the right platform as you are not aware of a well-developed trading style.

- In day trading, a trader doesn't need to trade all day. You will possibly discover more stability by only trading two to three hours a day.

- Make a note about your chart of profits/losses in pips (forex), points (futures), or cents (stocks) on a daily basis because these are scalable figures. Writing down dollar figures can make you confuse because there will be more chances that your account balance may fluctuate by the time, resulting in bigger or smaller trades.

- Save all the gathered data with a name, month-day-year.

- Make a folder on your computer and store the saved files over there for later reviews.

- Each weekend, go through the gathered data from the previous week.

- Note where you made a mistake and what you need to improve in yourself.

- Day traders should practice all the precise issues in a demo account during non-trading hours.

NOTE:

For having a good position in the market, the trader should find the repeating patterns that are making continually profit in the market.

Trading Platforms

A beginner always has the trading platform in his mind whenever he thinks to start trading where he should trade or not, which platform will be more beneficial for him. The future of trade is more often based on the indexes and commodities. A beginner could trade gold, crude oil, or S&P movements. Not every market is good; it changes and comes down to what you trade and what you can afford by the time. There are a lot of markets for trading that can help beginners in achieving their goals, but finding the right one to invest your money is very important. Day traders are admirable risk-takers. They take risks in that area where they can't afford to take risks. Still, they utilize this trading platform. Day traders must have a fast, reliable platform full of tools and features to ensure an optimal trading experience.

There are thousands of stocks in the market to choose, how do you decide which one will give you more profit or you are going to focus on for day trading? It can be confusing for a beginner trying to figure out the right one. Some day traders find easily new stocks to trade every day or hunt for stocks that are breaking out of patterns. Therefore, others lookout for stocks that breakout of support or resistance levels or are the most volatile. A beginner should keep these things in his mind while choosing a market, that when you have picked up a market for your investment, you should have the proper equipment and software setup, and knowledge about the goods for day trading. When you start thinking about trading, you need to know how to control risk. Day traders may control risk in two ways: trade risk and daily risk. Trade risk is how far you are willing to take the risk on each trade. Ideally, about risk 1% or less of your money on each trade.

A beginner can also start his trade with a little amount of $50, although if he can invest more than starting with more is recommended. Whereas some trading markets required $1,000 to get started. A day trader at least requires $25,000 to trade for his stock. The need for having more capitals to day trade stock will not make it better or worse in the market than the others. It is essential for trading to maintain your position good in the market for that you have to maintain your account up to $25,000, but if you are facing continual failure, then this market is not a good place for you.

3.SWING TRADING AND DAY TRADING: TACTICS AND STRATEGIES

What is strategy?

"Strategy is an action or plan that is used to attain one or more of the organizational aims."

A trading strategy is a procedure through which a trader sells and buys the stock and is based on predefined rules used to make trading decisions. Any type of trading process in the market usually includes a well-considered trading and investing plan that specifies risk tolerance, tax implication, and capitalizing objects. Applying or planning a strategy in trading means that a trader should search and adopt the best practices and ideas and then follows them.

REMINDER:

The strategy includes three stages:
Planning a trade, placing a trade, and then executing it.

A trader should understand the level of risk he can take and then decide what is appropriate for him to do. Trading strategies are mainly based on either fundamentals or methodological. To avoid behavioral finance biases and to make sure about consistent results, trading strategies are employed. Even though it is very difficult to develop a trading strategy because there are more chances of having a risk of becoming over-reliant on a strategy.

How many strategies does a trader need?

A trader should use only one or two strategies for successful trading. It is a pattern of buying and selling the stocks every trader uses in their daily routine, which outlines when a trader will enter and exit the market. The trading strategy allows the trader to see the trading opportunities objectively. It also allows the trader to see how the trades and traders have worked out in the past.

Types of strategies:

There are four types of trading styles.

1. Scalping.
2. Day trading.
3. Position trading.
4. Swing trading.

Trading styles, time frame and their time of a period frame are given below:

Trading Style	Time Frame	Time Period of Frame
Scalping	Short-term	Seconds or minutes

Day trading	Short-term	For one day (maximum)
Position trading	Long-term	Weeks, months, or years.
Swing Trading	Medium-term	Days or weeks

These trading styles are the four main types of trading mostly use in the forex market.

Day trading strategy

Day trading strategies are important for the trader when he is looking to capitalize on small price movements. A trading strategy helps the trader to understand how from thousands of stocks, a reader can decide or choose the right one. This book will help beginners to understand the market situation and helps in focusing on which strategy will help the trader. Sometimes beginners get confused due to their zero experience in the beginning, and they lose their hopes, but here we will try to end the confusion of the trading beginners before it actually begins in their minds. A consistent, effective strategy in day trading relies on utilizing charts, technical indicators, in-depth technical analysis, and patterns; it helps in predicting future price movements in trading. This book will give you a detailed breakdown of beginners' trading strategies. The fast step of moving investment positions in a single trading day creates a perception that day trading is riskier or extra volatile than other types of trading.

It is essential for a beginner to know the basic concept of trading because it could bog down a trader in a complex world of highly technical indicators, that's why focus and knowledge both are important for a simple day trading strategy. Having patience and control is very important for the day trader because there will be days when it will turn out to be ranging days in trading. One of the most common mistakes that every beginner usually makes is taking the risk of trading too early while knowing it can damage them financially, still trying to get a better price and position in the market and assuming that the trade will trigger them in the future. This is the biggest mistake that every beginner has usually made.

Basic strategic fundamentals every day trader should use:

- A trader should not expect to make a fortune if he is only allocating an hour or two a day to trading. A trader needs to continuously monitor the markets and keep looking for trading chances.

- Before you start doing trading, first, you need to decide how much you're prepared to take a risk. A trader should keep in mind that most successful traders won't put more than 2% of their investment on the line per trade.

- A trader should prepare himself for some losses if he wants to be around when the winner's start rolling in.

- A trader should make sure that he should stay up to date with the events and market news that will influence your asset, such as a shift in economic policy. A trader can discover a wealth of online economic and business resources that will keep them in the know.

- For trading, just having the knowledge of the market intricacies isn't enough; a trader should be informed about everything.

- The trading market will get volatile when it opens each day and while practiced day traders who are capable of reading the outlines and profit, a trader should bide his time

- It's tougher than it looks to keep your emotions at bay when you are five coffees in, and you have been watching at the screen for hours. A trader should let maths, logic, and the trading strategy guide him rather than nerves, fear, or greed.

- A trader must have technical tools in the beginning, but also the best place to experiment with new strategies for advanced traders is the demo account. Several demo accounts are unrestricted, so not time restriction.

Important Components for day trading:

Whether it is automated day trading strategies, or advanced tactics and beginner, a trader will need to take three essential components; liquidity, volatility, and volume. If a beginner wants to create money by making tiny price movements, choosing the right stock is vigorous. These three elements will help the trader to make a decision.

1. Liquidity:

This enables the trader to suddenly enter and exit trades at an eye-catching and stable price. Liquid commodity strategies, for example, crude oil, focus on gold, and natural gas, etc.

2. Volatility:

Through this, every beginner trader will get to know about their potential profit range. The larger the volatility, the larger profit or loss a trader may make. The cryptocurrency market is an example of high volatility.

3. Volume:

This measurement will help the beginner to know about how many times the stock/asset has been traded within a set period of time. For a day trader beginners, this is known as 'average daily trading volume.' High volume helps in knowing that there's significant interest in the asset or security. Growth in volume is often an indicator a price goes either up or down, is fast approaching.

How much risk is involved in day trading?

According to the experts of (OTA) Online Trading Academy, it is a reality that day trading situations managing in a single day are making it truly safer rather than riskier.

"One of the best ways to control risk is limiting the length of the trade. The longer you are in a position, the greater the likelihood is that price could move against you. By day trading, you eliminate overnight and weekend risk, especially when you trade markets that close, like stocks."

– Brandon Wendell, CMT

Because it is a fact that day traders don't hold their positions overnight, they usually avoid the probability of a surprise in an overseas market, unfavorable financial news, or an incomes report that comes out once the markets are closed. Even though after-hours trading is offered for numerous securities, the market is high, and it's possible that the position will *gap down* and open at a dramatically lower price the next day after a negative overnight experience.

In addition, day trading tends to give ease, not increase market volatility. Day traders are usually looking for their earnings in small price movements up or down. Their daily trades offer liquidity, which helps the marketing the running easily, as compared to casually traded markets that are subject to dramatic price swings. Day trading is not a way to become rich instantly. Day trading is a traditional investing approach that is used by many organizations as well by the well-educated institutions who have adopted it as a profession.

In the 1990s, day trading did not have a good reputation, and at that time, many beginners began day trading. They started jumping into different platforms, including online trading platforms, without applying the stock strategies. They believed that they could run the market without having the knowledge about the market and make a fortune in stock trades with their little effort. This proved them wrong.

What do you need to start day trading?

For a day trader beginner, it is important to have technical equipment at your place. Most of the beginners think that daily trading requires heavy and expensive equipment and high investments of capital; that's not the reality.

Here's a list of items usually every trader needs for trading.

Technology:

For trading, traders do not want a supercharged computer with a dozen monitors to trade. They only need one laptop or a computer.

Internet Connection:

It is very important to have a good internet connection; it helps the trader to process his order in a timely manner. Most cables and even satellites suppliers offer sufficient bandwidth to connect to the exchanges. Typical packages of 20mbps of cable internet are enough for this. Most of the traders even use their mobile phone connections of 5mbps to 20mbps, but that is not suggested. The slow mobile phone connection can cause delays in transactions and can cause unexpected loss.

Trading Platform:

Traders should be careful in the trading market because there are many online brokers sitting online to fool the beginners. They offer the beginners their services but route orders over market makers who cost additional money, they often deferral the processing. It is easy to perform trade analysis and place your orders very quickly and properly. The web-based version is less reliable then the downloaded version, the downloaded version offers more features.

Skills

Lots of people are supporters of seeking an education. The main problem is that; education alone is not enough unless it is being utilized rightly in the market. Although having information about the markets, how it will work, and how to read price is essential, and how it will offer an advantage, skill is also necessary to obtain stable results.

Building a skill involves practice and experience, but trying to get trading skills without supervision can be a lengthy, often annoying process. For many traders, working and learning from the experience of a counselor is the best way to improve any of the skills and learn strategies for trading and investing that reduces risk. Even the famous traders like Paul Tudor and Warren Buffett Jones needed mentors. Mr. Buffett worked under Benjamin Graham, and Mr. Jones worked under Eli Tullis.

Day Trading Strategies

Strategies

1. Breakout

In trading breakout strategies center around after the price clears a specified level on the chart, with improved volume. The breakout trader enters into a long situation once the security or asset breaks above resistance. Otherwise, a trader enters a short site after the stock breaks below support.

Once a security or asset trades beyond the quantified amount barrier, volatility frequently increases, and the amount will often trend in the way of the breakout.

A trader needs to catch the right instrument to trade. While doing this, bear in the notice the resistance level and asset's support. The more often the price has hit these facts, the more authenticated and vital they become.

Plan the Entry and Exits Points:

This part of trading is good and direct. Prices set to nearby and above resistance levels want a bearish place. Prices set to nearby and below a maintenance level want a bullish place.

Using the asset's latest performance to establish a sensible price target. Using chart patterns in trading will make this process even more precise. A trader can analyze the average current price swings to generate a target. If the average swings have been 3 points over the last some price swings, this would be a workable target. Once you've got hold of that goal, then you can exit the trade and enjoy the profit.

2. Scalping

Scalping is one of the best strategies, mostly used by traders. It is mostly used, and it is popular in the forex market. It looks to capitalize on minute price changes, and its driving force is quantity. You will look to sell the stock as soon as the stock becomes profitable. This is an exciting and fast-paced technique to trade, but then again, it can be risky. You must have a high trading probability to even out the reward ratio vs. low risk. A trader should be on the lookout for volatile tools, attractive liquidity, and be on timing. You cannot wait for the market; you must close losing trades as soon as possible.

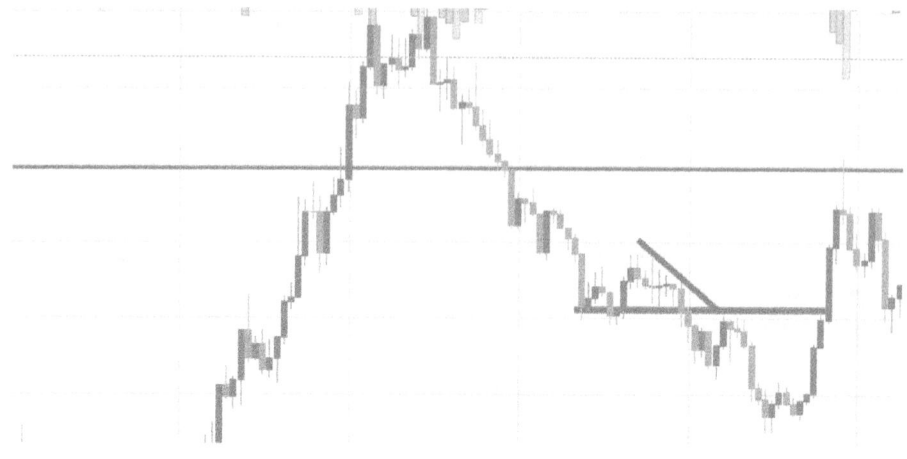

3. Momentum:

This strategy is popular among all trading strategies for beginners; this strategy revolves around acting on recognizing large trending moves with the support of high volume and news sources. For the ample opportunity, there is always at least one stock that moves around 20-30% each day. A trader simply holds onto the position until he sees signs of reversal and then gets out. Otherwise, he can disappear the price drop. This way round his price target as soon as volume starts to shrink.

This is the simplest and most effective strategy if used properly. However, a trader must ensure that he is aware of upcoming news and income announcements. Just a small number of seconds on each trade will make all the difference to your end of day profits.

4. Reversal

Though this strategy is hotly debated and potentially unsafe when it comes to using by beginners. Reverse trading is used all over the world. It's also known as pullback trending, trend trading, and a mean reversion strategy. This strategy confronts the basic logic as the trader aims to trade against the trend. A trader must be able to correctly classify possible pullbacks, plus calculate their strength. To do this effectively, a trader must need in-depth market experience and knowledge.

The 'daily pivot' strategy is measured as a unique case of reverse trading, as it centers on selling and buying the daily high and low pullbacks/reverse.

5. Using Pivot Points

A day trading pivot point strategy can be strange or fantastic in trading for acting on critical support and/or resistance levels identifying it. It is mostly useful in the forex market. In addition, pivot points can be used by range-bound traders to recognize points of entry, whereas trend and breakout traders can use pivot points to locate key levels that must break a move to count as a breakout.

Calculating Pivot Points

A pivot point is well-defined as a point of rotation in day trading. A beginner day trader can use the prices of the previous day's low or high and, plus the closing price of a security to analyze the pivot point.

Note that if you analyze a pivot point using price statistics from a quite short time frame, accuracy is often reduced.

So, how does a day trader will analyze/calculate the pivot point?

> ➢ Central Pivot Point (P) = (High + Low + Close) / 3

Now day traders can analyze resistance and support levels by using the pivot point. For doing that a trader must use the following formulas:

> ➢ First Resistance (R1) = (2*P) – Low
> ➢ First Support (S1) = (2*P) – High

The second level of resistance and support is then calculated as follows:

> ➢ Second Resistance (R2) = P + (R1-S1)
> ➢ Second Support (S2) = P – (R1- S1)

Application

When practically applied in the FX market, for example, a beginner will find the trading range for the session that will frequently take place among the pivot point and the resistance levels and the first support. The reason behind this is having a high number of traders playing this range. It is also worth noting because this is one of the systems &approaches that can be applied to indexes too.

For example, it can help a day trader beginner to form an effective S&P day trading strategy.

Limit Your Losses

This is the most important thing to keep in your mind if you are using a margin is limiting your loss. Requirements are often high for day traders. When a day trader trades on a margin, he will be increasingly susceptible to sharp price movements. This means the potential for a bigger profit, but it also means the probability of substantial losses. Luckily, a trader can employ stop-losses. The stop-loss controls the trade risk for the trader. In a small situation, a trader can place a stop-loss above a recent high; for good big situations, you can place it below a recent low. A trader can also make it dependent on volatility.

For example, if a stock amount moves by £0.05 a minute, so you can place a stop-loss £0.15 away after your entry order, letting it swing (hopefully in the expected direction).

One popular strategy in day trading is to set up two stop-losses. Firstly, a trader places a physical stop-loss order at a precise price level. This will be the maximum capital you can afford to lose. Secondly, you can create a mental stop-loss. Place this, at the point of your entry criteria, are breached. So if the trade makes an unexpected turn, you'll make a swift exit.

Forex Trading Strategies

Forex strategies are risky by nature as a trader must accumulate his profits in a short space of time. A trader can apply any of the strategies in the forex market.

Swing trading strategy

What is a swing trader?

Swing traders are basically those traders that trade for a couple of days or for weeks' time frame. They usually work for four hours (H4) and daily (D1) charts, and they may use a blend of fundamental analysis and technical analysis to monitor trading their decisions. Whether it is a long term trend or whether the market is mainly range-bound, it really does not matter. A Forex swing trader is not going to hold on to a position that is enough for it to count considerably.

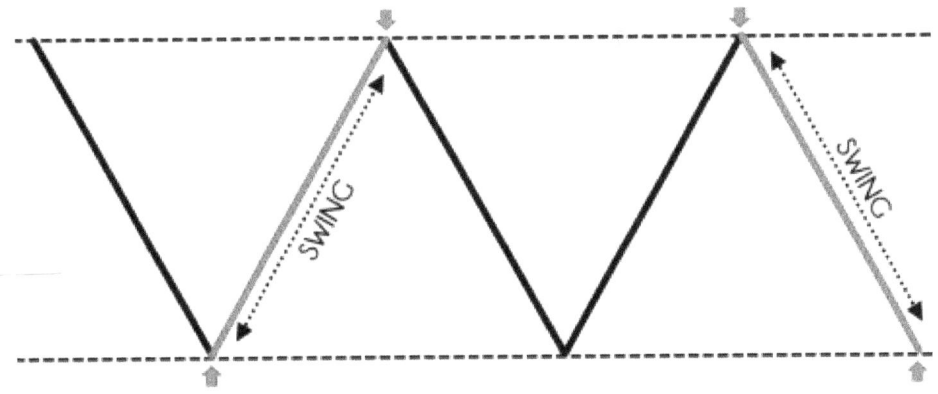

In the trading market, the swing trader is best to be used when markets are going nowhere once indexes rise for multi-days, then decay for the next few days, only to repeat the same over-all patterns again and again. Swing trader has several chances to catch the short-term movements up and down. The problem with swing trading and long-term trend trading is that success is established on correctly recognizing what type of market is presently being practiced. Trend trading might have the perfect strategy for the bull market of the 1990s, while swing trading maybe would have been best for 2000 and 2001.

Simple moving averages (SMAs) offer resistance and support levels, as well as bearish and bullish patterns. Support and resistance levels can help the trader in buying a stock. Bullish and bearish limit patterns signal price ideas where you should enter and exit stocks. The exponential moving average (EMA) is similar to SMA that places extra emphasis on the latest data points. The EMA gives traders clear trend indications, entry, and exit points faster than a simple moving average (SMA). Swing trades can use EMA for entry and exit points.

A swing trader tends to look for multi-day chart outlines. Some of the more common outlines include moving average crossovers, head and shoulders patterns, flags, triangles, and cup-and-handle patterns. Eventually, each swing trader formulates a plan and strategy that gives them an advantage over many trades. This also includes looking for trade arrangements that tend to lead to expectable movements in the asset's price. This is not that easy, and no strategy or any arrangement will work every time. Through a favorable risk or reward, winning every time is not required. The more promising risk or reward of a trading strategy, the fewer times it desires to win in order to produce a complete profit over many trades.

Once it comes to take profits, the swing traders, whether they are beginners or the professionals, they will want to exit the trade as soon as possible to the upper or lower channel line without being too defined, which can cause the risk of missing the finest opportunity.

In the book of Dr. Alexander Elder, "Come Into My Trading Room: A Complete Guide to Trading" (2002), he uses his understanding of a stock's behavior above and below the baseline to define the swing trader's strategy of "buying regularity and selling mania" or "shorting regularity and covering depression." Once the swing trader used the EMA to recognize the typical baseline on the stock chart, the trader goes long at the baseline once the stock is heading up and short at the baseline once the stock is on its way down.

Therefore, swing traders are not looking to smash the home run by a single trade; they are not alarmed with the perfect time to purchase a stock exactly at its bottom and sell exactly at its top. In a perfect trading environment, beginners should wait for the stock to hit its baseline and confirm its way before they make their moves. The story becomes more complex when a tougher uptrend or downtrend is at play. The trader may unexpectedly go long once the stock dips below its EMA and pause for the stock to go back up in an uptrend, or a trader may short a stock that has stuck above the EMA and wait for it to drop if the time-consuming trend is down.

NOTE:

Many traders believe that they cannot make trades by greater as their account is too small.

If a trader is calculating his position before each trade and risking a similar amount in each trade, then a trader ought to be able to play a trade whether the stop is 60 pips or 10.

Popular Swing Trading Strategies:

Swing trading is frequently done within trends, and this is a common way; it can also be successfully carried out in ranging markets. A swing trader analyses the price profit and action from the greater part of the market's next swing. The markets spend far-off extra of their time reaching; then they do create clear trends higher or lower and being capable to successfully trade ranging markets, is critical.

Forex Swing Trading Strategies:

Swing trading is not a strategy; it is a style. The time frame of swing trading describes this style, and within that, there are unlimited strategies that we can use to swing trade. Swing trading is a style that works over short to moderate time frames. Swing trading style lies between the very long time frames of position trading and short time frames of day trading. It is not so short that it requires all your time observing the market, yet it is short enough to offer plenty of trading chances. These strategies are not limited to swing trading; it is the case with most technical strategies, support and resistance are the ideas behind them.

These concepts can give a trader two choices within the swing trading strategy with, following the trend, or trading counter to the trend. Counter trending strategies aim to profit once support and resistance levels hold up. Trend following strategies looks for the chances when support and resistance levels break down.

For trading swing traders can use the following strategies for actionable trading opportunities:

Swing trading strategy 1: Trend trading

When classifying a trend, it's essential to recognize that markets don't tend to move in a straight line. Even while eventually trending, they move up and down in step like moves. A trader should recognize an uptrend by the market, making higher highs and higher lows, and a downtrend by recognizing lower lows and lower highs. Many swing trading strategies of trying to catch and follow a short trend.

Swing trading strategy 2: Counter-trend trading

The next swing trading strategy is counter-trend trading and therefore does the reverse of the first one. We practice the similar principles in terms of trying to spot relatively short-term trends from building, but now try to profit as of the frequency with which these trends tend to break down.

NOTE:

Uptrend = Higher lows and Higher highs

Downtrend = Lower lows and lower highs

A counter-trend trader would effort to catch the swing in this period of reversion. Therefore, the trader would try to identify the break in the trend. In an uptrend, this might be a fresh high was followed by a series of failures to break new highs. Hence we go short in expectation of such a reversion. The reverse is true in a downtrend.

Itis very important to maintain a strong discipline encounter trending if the price travels against you, and if the market resumes its trend against you, then you should be ready to admit that you are wrong, and you had drawn a line under the trade.

Swing trading strategy 3: A versatile swing trading strategy

If a trader would like to take an even deeper dive into swing trading, besides learning a multipurpose strategy that even beginners can use. Being a versatile trader means that a trader is able to trade any instrument, in any timeframe or in any direction.

Improving swing trading strategies for beginners:

What swing can traders do to increase their strategies?

There are numerous things a trader can try. The first thing is to effort to match the trade with the long-term trend. While the hourly chart helps the swing trader to also look at a longer-term chart to get a feel for the long-standing trend. Try and trade merely once your direction matches whatever you see as the long-term trend. Another way to recover your swing trading strategy is to use a technical indicator to confirm your thinking.

A moving average (MA) is one more indicator you can use to help. An MA flattens the prices to give a clearer view of the trend. And because an MA includes older price data, it's an easy way to match how the recent prices compare to older prices.

Managing risk in Forex swing trading:

Have you ever read about trading Forex and that the widely held of traders that lost money because of it? Have you ever understood that this is even true for successful traders?

The reality is that no trader wins 100% of the time. Most of the time it happens that the beginners of the swing trading misjudge the market, sometimes it moves unexpectedly, sometimes the trader might just make a mistake. This is the point where risk management and money management are so important.

In trading, but especially in Forex, a trader should know how to lose before knowing how to get success. And when traders talk about having enough knowledge on how to lose, he should also know how to lose tiny to win big. Basically, if a trader can achieve a swing trading risk, then he can close out losing trades early, which will help to ensure he enjoys extra profits than losses.

Some tips for handling your risk in swing trading include:

1. Maximum acceptable loss:

In spite of the fact that a trade clearly wants his next trade to make a profit, it's important to think through the supreme amount you are prepared to lose on a trade. The minute a trader knows this amount can set a stop loss to close his trade spontaneously if it travels too far in the incorrect direction then this will help to protect him when he can't automatically be at your computer observing every trade.

2. Taking a risk on any one trade:

No matter what is the size of your trading account, you must avoid risking your whole balance on a trade. If a trader does not follow that, then he can possibly lose it all. Andover-all rule is not to risk more than 2% of your account balance on any one trade.

3. Increasing account balance to diversify risk:

Despite the fact that a trader might be able to open an account from as little as €300, it is better to start using a larger sum. This means that a trader will have an adequate amount of your account to trade a diversity of assets and expand the risk of swing trading. Swing trading is by description a long-term investment style, so you need extra verge on your places to manage with market explosive nature.

4. Information about your profile:

One of the first and most important things to do when you start trading in the market is to understand your risk aversion and volatility. In other words, at what stage of the loss will a trader starts to panic? If a swing trader has an account balance of €25,000 and he has lost €3,000, then this means that the trader has lost 10% of his capital. In that case, would he be a failure, or would he think through that to be usual? How the trader will respond to this loss will influence the risks he is willing to take in trading.

You can see that this strategy will be easy for a beginner to understand. Therefore, a Swing Trading strategy is an average and long-term trading strategy. This strategy is very dependent on the capital and management of risks. It is most commonly called money management swing trading.

Swing trading money management:

Once a trader understands the big picture of the trading after that, he still has to manage his risk every day in the market. And one way to do trading wisely is by managing your money successfully. It might give the impression like a complex question, but in reality, it doesn't have to be.

For example: If a trader wanted to keep the total risk of 6% of his account balance so he could have six trades opened, each risking 1% of his assets.

For that reason, a trader could lose 1% of his capital in six different trades or a maximum amount of €200 in each trade if you had an account of €20,000. At that point, before taking a position, a trader should be aware of his maximum risk for proper management of his assets in Swing Trading that will be 1% or 200 euros. For that reason, your stop-loss and neutralization position will be determined previously by each position. And from there, you should perform as many actions as you can without overcoming your risk management.

That boundary will then affect your actions, and you will close since the trade is approaching your loss limit, or you will lose the trade because the asset goes up and reaches the target profit. And if a trade passes the breakeven fact, at which point it develops a 'neutral' trade, you can take on a new site, without endangering your risk limit.

The best tools for swing trading:

There is a range of tools a trader can use to improve his chances of success while performing swing trading strategies.

Some ranges that are recommended:

- **Correlation Matrix:** The relationship between Forex pairs, supplies, or stock guides is one element of analysis that allows sensible trading to trade with self-confidence.

- **Mini Charts**:

A mini charting tool permits the trader to analyze numerous units of time on a single chart. Which means that there is no need for the trader to shift from swing chart W1 to D1 to come to be on the H4 chart to discover his entry point

- **Symbol Info:**

In the same manner, this Forex swing indicator lets traders understand on a single chart the trading signals of the maximum used indicators on eight different interval scales.

- **Mini Terminal:**

The mini terminal tool allows the trader to open a place in Meta Trader in a second, but then again, it also permits the swing trader to open trades regarding the risk in permanent euros or in percentage. In fact, it provides you with diverse information associated with the stock market or the currency pair in which a trader can apply it, including the current trend, the strength of current movements and current momentum

Other useful indicators for swing traders include are:

- Exponential Mobile Average

- MACD

- Overwhelming oscillator

- Parabolic SAR

- CCI

- Admiral Donchian

So here comes the question that troubles the beginners, that from where the beginners of swing trading can access these swing trading tools? It's easy for those who have a demo or a live account with Admiral Markets. And if not, then the good news is that any of the beginners can easily access these totally free with Meta-Trader Supreme Edition.

Meta-Trader Supreme Edition is an absolutely free plugin for MT4 and MT5 that contains a range of unconventional features, such as an indicator package with technical analysis trading ideas provided by Trading Central, and 16 new indicators and mini terminals and mini charts to mark your trading even more effectual.

Top tips for Forex swing trading for beginners:

After knowing the basics of the swing, and after having enough information about the Forex swing trading strategies, here are the top tips that will help you to succeed as a swing trader.

1. Match your trades by the long-term trend:

Although a trader may always be looking at a time chart of shorter-term (e.g., H1 or H4), it may also comfort the beginner to look at a longer-term chart (D1 or W1) to get the information about the long-term trend. Then you can make sure that you aren't trading beside a larger trend. Swing trading is also much easier when it's been trading by means of the trend, rather than against the trend.

2. Make the best of Moving Averages (MAs):

The MA indicator may profit the trader to classify trends by moderating shorter-term price differences. Since the MA comprises old data prices, it is the easiest way to associate what way the existing price links with older prices.

3. Use a little leverage:

Leverage lets the trader access a larger position than it would usually let your deposit, together with strengthening your profits and losses. Once used wisely, leverage can help the trader to make the most of winning trades.

4. Trade a wide-ranging portfolio of Forex pair:

Lookout as several currency pairs as you can to discover the best opportunities. The Forex market will every time offer you trading opportunities you want; you need to look for the ones that match best with your signal. Plus, trading a range of pairs will support to diversify your portfolio, and achieve the risk of having all your eggs in one basket.

5. Pay attention to swaps:

Swaps are a cost of trading concern charge ready for positions held overnight. These swaps need to be taken into account in swing trading of the trader in order to be able to manage your money better.

6. Maintaining a positive profit/loss ratio:

Whether it is H4 or daily trading, swing trading allows the trader to tap into large market schedules, giving the trader the chance to get larger profit ratios associated with very small losses possible, especially when matched to scalping.

7. Put a side your sentiments:

It's better to trade without emotions, but then again, to make swing trades as a part of a fixed Forex trading plan and strategy.

Choose a Broker for Forex Swing:

Before a trader starts trading, a trader needs to choose a broker. Choosing a broker for the Forex market will give a chance to the new traders to access the markets in a way that wants to trade, along with a trading platform to carry out his trades. Though some brokers are better than others, that's why it is essential to keep the following in mind while making a choice.

- Check if they are synchronized by the local regulator in your area? Admiral Markets is a Forex and CFD broker that is controlled by the EFSA, ASIC CYSEC, and FCA.

- The costs of trading contain the spread, the swap, and orders on trades, which know how to eat into your profits. That's why it is essential to have knowledge about typical trading costs.

- A standard Forex share, or trading contract, is value 100,000 of the base currency of the pair before the first currency listed (if one share of the EUR/USD costs EUR 100,000). For new traders, this might be extra than you want to see, so check whether the broker deals micro (0.01) and mini (0.1) lots for trading.

- To make knowledgeable trading decisions, it is essential to have the latest market information. Good Forex and CFD brokers will deal with live price facts in their trading platform.

- The next point is having knowledge about the market and how much leverage does the broker offer? If you talk about Europe, in Europe, the brokers should offer access to leverage up to 1:500 for Specialized Clients and 1:30 for Retail Customers.

- What is the least amount a trader needs to start trading? At Admiral Markets, a trader can supply the trading account with as little as €100. This also allows the trader to start small trade without taking a major risk and add as you learn the market psychology and behavior of self-governing trading.

- Admiral Markets can support the trader to decrease his trading risk with volatility defense and negative balance protection.

- Will, the broker, let the trader not simply swing trade, but day trade and scalp as well, if that's a part of the strategy?

- Does the broker in swing trading provide tools and resources to help the beginner to succeed as a trader? As if we talk about Admiral Markets, for example, it has a library of more than hundreds of Forex articles, free courses like Forex 101, and free trading webinars.

Forex Swing Trading Strategies

A Summary

Swing trading is a style suitable for volatile markets, and it also suggests frequent trading chances. Though the trader will need to capitalize a reasonable amount of time into observing the market with swing trading, the supplies are not as difficult as trading styles with smaller time frames, such as day trading or scalping. In calculation, even if you give favor to day trade or scalping, swing trading will offer you few diversifications in your outcomes as well as additional profits. It is said that swing trading is not for all traders, so it is best to practice it with risk-free first with a demo trading account.

Admiral Markets:

Admiral Markets is a market that has attained many successes in the market due to its multi-award-winning achievement. Forex and CFD broker, providing trading on over 8,000 financial instruments via the world's most popular trading platforms:

1.MetaTrader 4

2.MetaTrader 5

This substantial does not hold and should not be construed as containing asset advice, asset recommendations, an offer of or solicitation for any dealings in financial instruments. A beginner should not forget that such trading analysis is not a trustworthy indicator for any current or future performance, as conditions may change over time. Before making any investment conclusions, he should seek guidance from independent financial advisors to confirm that you understand the risks.

4. SWING AND DAY TRADING INDICATORS

What are the indicators of trading?

"Trading indicators are the mathematical calculations, that are designed to predict what market will do."

Trading indicators are plotted as lines on a price chart and may comfort traders to identify certain signals and trends within the market. The number one indicator could be a forecast signal that calculates future price movements, while a lagging indicator looks at past trends and indicates momentum.

Why Are Technical Indicators Important?

Technical indicators are supported algorithms that practice previous price-data in the calculation. As an outcome, all technical indicators of trading are lagging in their natural surroundings, but that doesn't mean that they can't return useful information once day trading the markets. Deprived of the assistance of indicators, traders would have a tough time calculating this volatility of the markets, the strength of a trend, or whether market conditions are overbought or oversold.

That being said, an entire trading strategy shouldn't be dependent solely on technical indicators. They return the simplest results as a confirmation tool. Don't buy just because the RSI is below 30 or sell because the Stochastics oscillator increases directly above 80. As an alternative, a trader should create a definite trading strategy (built on price-action or the fundamentals, for instance) and using technical indicators simply to substantiate a possible setup and modify your entry levels.

Types of Technical Indicators

Depending on the knowledge that technical indicators provide, they'll be grouped into three main categories:

Trend-following indicators.

Momentum indicators.

Volatility indicators.

1. Trend-following indicators

Trend-following indicators are accustomed to determine trends and to live the strong point of a trending market. While most traders are able to identify a trend just by staring at the value chart, it's often difficult to live its strength or to identify a trend early in its establishment. The common trend-following indicators also contain moving averages, MACD, and also the ADX indicator, to call some.

2. Momentum indicator:

It usually measures the strength of recent price-moves relative to previous periods. They vary in the middle of 0 and 100, on condition of the signals of the indicator of overbought and oversold market circumstances. Momentum indicators return a marketing signal when values begin to maneuver strongly higher, and a buying signal when prices start to maneuver strongly lower. While this will be profitable in ranging markets, momentum indicators usually return false signals during strong trends. Some samples of momentum indicators include the RSI, Stochastics, and CCI.

3. Volatility indicators:

Volatility indicators, as per their name recommends, it measures the volatility of the fundamental instrument. Traders are generally chasing volatility from corner to different corner markets to hunt out profitable trading opportunities, which makes volatility indicators a strong tool for day trading. Samples of volatility indicators include Bollinger Bands and also the ATR indicator, among others.

Every investor has faith in the strategy of buying and holding. The only topic of disputation is how long the holding era should last. For every teenager who started buying unappreciated equity and holds it for eight decades, collecting shares along the way, there are dozens of more risk-takers who dearth to get out of their positions in less than a week. This not only requires a stock to rise quickly but also to go up in price high sufficient to offset any matter costs. Swing trading is for the stockholder who factually can't wait for the weekend.

Swing trading is the most fast-paced trading process that is manageable for everyone, even those beginners who have just jumped into the world of trading. The speed of swing trading is slower than day trading, which also delivers the trader with sufficient time to formulate a practice and execute a little research before building decisions on your trade. Swing trading is also a rare method for those looking to create a foray into day trading to increase their skills before embarking on the extra complex day trading process.

Those technical indicators are the mathematical tools that can give actionable info out of a stock plan that can seem uninformed at times. In the hands of an appropriately lucky risk-taker, the right technical indicators can spell a chance for profit. Now, just a rare of the ones most commonly used by swing traders, in ascending order of complexity.

Swing traders tend to have not the same goals as day traders, which goal to pick up on rapid intraday changes due to a catalyst.

Swing trades, on the other hand, tend to goal for "swings" moving from a short-term low back to a new high.

Swing trading signals tend to look not the same as day trading signals. Day traders frequently look for high volatility and volume and look to ride a trend, possibly buying at a pullback to VWAP.

Before we talk about the trading indicators, it is essential to understand what they represent and why and how they represent it are also important questions to think. Swing trading indicators are not better than any other method of technical analysis, and it should certainly not have seen as the divine grail. It is not assured that any trade that a trader makes will yield profit just for the reason that a trading indicator signaled it.

Here are few other factors that can have an influence on whether you end up creating a profit or bearing a loss in swing trading:

- Market Conditions can frequently reduce the effectiveness of indicators. Even if it appears like security is nearby to go up, a broad bearish emotion could cause it to additional fall in value.

- The timing of your trade needs to be rigorous. Receiving the right time can be authoritative to create a huge profit.

- What many people call perception is simply know-how. Like all other things, you will turn out to be a better trader as you spend extra time trading and pick up on subtle market signals.

Swing Trading Indicators:

Swing trade indicators are important to focus on when selecting when to buy when to trade, and what to buy. Some of the top combinations of indicators for swing trading are given below.

1. Moving Averages:

The moving average is one of the foremost basic trading indicators in swing trading. A moving average smoothens erratic short-term price movements and comforts us to better understand the trend and in what way the safety is moving. Moving Averages are good indicators on their own, but they are also used as a base for other, more descriptive indicators. Swing trader should not forget this that moving averages approximately always lag behind the present price thanks to factoring in past data. The more data you think about, the larger the lag. Therefore, as a swing trader. It is smart to mix short term moving averages with longer-term moving averages. Doing so, you think about both the long and short term trend and have more ground on which to base your decisions.

When a trader is observing at moving averages, he will be observing at the calculated lines built on past prices. This indicator is not difficult to understand, and it is also difficult to look at whether you are doing day trading, swing trading, or else even trading longer term. They are used to either confirm a trend or identify a trend. To decide the average, a trader will need to sum up all of the concluding prices as well as the number for days the period covers and then divide the concluding prices via the number of days. To successfully use moving averages, a trader will need to compute different time periods and link them on a chart. This will give the trader a broader lookout of the market, as well as their average changes over time. When you have planned your moving averages, you then must use them to consider in on your trade decisions. You can practice them to:

- **Recognize the Strength of a Trend:**

If the present price of the stock and trend is beyond from its moving average, then it is considered to be a weaker trend. Trend strength, shared by an indicator like volume, can help you create better choices on your trades.

- **Determining Trend Reversals:**

You can use moving averages to recognize trend reversals with limits. You need to watch for instances where the current moving averages cross the longer moving averages after an uptrend. Though this is not the only instrument, you should use to regulate reversal, but it can comfort you to determine whether you should explore it further.

2. Relative Strength Index:

Welles Wilder developed the RSI indicator within the 1970s and distributed his findings in New Concepts in Technical Trading Systems. The book may be a classic text which presented multiple conventional technical indicators like RSI, Average True Range, and, therefore, the Average Directional Index. A simple explanation of RSI's calculation is linking this price strength relative to past price strength. For instance, a 14-period RSI on a daily chart will compare today's price to the last 13 closes. A high reading points out that today's price is powerful, relative to the previous 13 closes, and contrariwise. Wilder planned that RSI could be used as a momentum oscillator: measuring exactly how tough the momentum is during a market, but then RSI came to be used in a different way. RSI is mostly used by the traders as an overbought-oversold indicator, where a great reading means that the stock is "overbought" and is unavoidable for a pullback. In the comparison, an "oversold" reading indicates that the market is due for a rally because it's been sold-off an excessive amount of. This consumption of the indicator compares to the aim of a momentum oscillator, contained by which a great analysis indicates that this trend is further likely to last. In the conventional time series of 14-period RSI is used. The situation is the one suggested in also Wilders' work and is defaulting in maximum charting platforms. On the other hand, the study of Larry Connors's point towards the 14-period RSI comprises a miniature edge, in which shorter-term RSI analyses produce additional commercial signals.

Connors' research indicates that the 2, four, and blended RSI periods show the most effective long-term trade expectation. As a result of his research, Connors developed the Connors RSI indicator (which measures the speed of change of RSI), which is included with most charting packages nowadays.

Relative strength index (RSI) is one of the finest technical indicators for swing trading. This indicator is responsible for giving the information you need to determine once the ideal enters into the market. It allows traders to investigate small signals better. This will help the trader to regulate if the market has been oversold or overbought, is range-bound, or is flat. The RSI will give the trader a relative evaluation of how to secure the existing price by examining both past instability and performance. This indicator will be easily recognized by using a range of 1-100. The RSI indicator is most convenient for:

- **Determining the circumstances that led the market to oversold or overbought:**

A trader will need to be able to classify these conditions so that a trader can find equally trend reversal and corrections. Overbuying can indicate a bearish trend even though overselling can be seen as more bullish. If the indicator is around 30, it could be indicated as an undervalue or oversold. Indicators about 70 may mean that the security was overrated or overbought.

- **Identifying Divergences:**

Divergences are used to classify reversals in trends. When the value hits a new low, but then the RSI does not, then at that time, it would be considered as a bullish divergent signal. If the value hits a new high and the RSI doesn't, then that would be termed a bearish signal.

3. Volume:

A generally overlooked indicator that is easiest for beginners to use, even for new traders, is volume. Looking at volume is very critical when you are considering trends. Trends need to be maintained and supported by volume. A trader always wants to make sure that there is more significant volume going on when the trend is going in that way. Increasing volume means money supporting the safety, and if you do not see the volume, it may possibly be an indication that there are undervalued conditions at play.

4. Visual Analysis Indicator:

Despite the fact that technical indicators for swing trading are critical for making the right choices, it is helpful from many shareholders, both new and experienced, to be able to look at visual patterns. By generating visuals patterns, a trader can see the activities in the market with a quick glance to help support your decision.

5. The Flow of Net Imbalances:

Each day, there are a lot of orders to be found to urge the closing print (market-on-close orders). These are typically institutions like mutual funds and ETFs that need the large liquidity provided at the market close. Some minutes before they close every day, the interactions will distribute information on the order inequalities at the market close. That is, what number more shares are being accepted than sold at the close? For instance, if market-on-close buy orders are equaling 100,000 shares, and sell orders equaling 90,000 shares, that's a +10,000 share imbalance. Market makers arbitrage this within the short-term and make pennies, that's not a timeframe we are able to compete in. However, we are able to track the cash flow of a stock or sector by tracking the trend of the online imbalances over time.

If there are determined in closing the imbalances in one sector, it's indicating that institutions are collecting an edge therein stock. This provides us vital information that a major price move could be on the precipice. The tool I exploit to measure imbalance money flow is Market Chameleon. MC allows you to easily view 20-days or 50-days moving averages of capital inflows and outflows of sectors, industries, indexes, or watch lists.

Day Trading Indicators:

To find the simplest technical indicators for your particular day-trading approach, test out a bunch of them singularly and so together. You will find yourself sticking with, say, four that are evergreen otherwise, you may flip counting on the asset you're trading or the market situations of the day. Regardless of whether you are day-trading stocks, forex, or futures, it's often best to stay it simple when it involves technical indicators. You will find you like viewing only a pair of indicators to endorse entry points and exit points. At most, use simply one from each type of indicator to dodge avoidable and distracting repetition.

Combining Day-Trading Indicators

Consider a combination of sets of two indicators on your expense chart to classify points to initiate and get hold of out of a trade.

For example, Relative strength index RSI and moving average convergence/divergence will be combined on the screen to recommend and strengthen a trading signal. The relative strength index (RSI) can recommend overbought or oversold conditions by measuring the value momentum of an asset. The indicator was produced by J. Welles Wilder Jr, who proposed the momentum reaching 30 (on a scale of zero to 100) was an indication of an asset being oversold, and so a buying chance and a 70 percent level was an indication of an asset is overbought and so a selling or short-selling chance.

Constance Brown, CMT, refined the service of the index and assumed the oversold level in an exceedingly upward-trending market was fundamentally much above 30, and therefore, the overbought level in a downward-trending market was much below 70.3.Using Wilder's levels, the asset price can still trend higher for a few times, whereas the RSI is signifying overbought and the other way around. For that reason,

RSI is best monitored only if its signal imitates to the value trend: as an example, hunt for bearish momentum indications when the value trend is bearish and pay no attention to those indications when the value trend is bullish.

To more easily identify those price trends, you'll be able to use the moving average convergence/divergence (MACD) indicator. MACD consists of two chart lines. The MACD line is made by eliminating a 26-period exponential moving average (EMA) from a 12-period EMA. An EMA is that the average value of an asset over a period of your time only with the key change that the foremost recent prices are given greater allowance than prices farther out.

The second line is the signal line and could be a 9-period EMA. A bearish trend is signaled once the MACD line crosses under the signal line; a bullish trend is signaled after the MACD line crosses directly above the signal line.

Choosing Pairs:

While selecting pairs, it is a good knowledge to decide on one indicator that's measured a number one indicator, i.e., RSI and one that's a lagging indicator, i.e., like MACD. Most important indicators make signals before the conditions for entering the trade have arisen. Lagging indicators make warning signs after those circumstances have looked as if, in order that they can act as verification of leading indicators and might prevent you from trading on made-up signals.

A trader must also first-rate a pairing that features indicators as of two of the four different types, never two of the same type. The four types are development like MACD, moments like RSI, volatility, and volume. As their names suggest, volatility indicators are supported volatility within the asset's price, and volume indicators are supported trading volumes of the asset. It's typically not useful to look at two indicators of the identical type since they'll be on condition that the identical information.

Using Multiple Indicators:

A trader might also opt to have live one indicator of every type; it might possibly be two of which are maximum substantial and two of which are lagging. Numerous indicators can provide even more strengthening of trading signals and might increase your probabilities of hunting down made-up signals.

Refining Indicators:

Whatsoever indicators you choose, make sure to research them, and take summaries on their effectiveness over time. Ask yourself: What are an indicator's disadvantages? Does it produce several made-up signals? Does it fail to signal, leading to missed chances? Does it signal too early (more probable of a number one indicator) or too late (more likely of a lagging one)?

You may find one indicator is actual when trading stocks but not, say, forex. You may want to switch out an indicator for an additional one amongst its type or make changes in how it's planned. Making such modifications could be a key part of success when day-trading with technical indicators.

Should You Trade on Technical Indicators?

Technical indicators practice past price-data in their calculation and, as a result, lagging this price. On the other hand, since historical data is that the only piece of knowledge that traders must do in advance for future price movements, technical indicators do have a very important role during a well-defined trading strategy.

Avoiding the addition of too adding too many indicators to your chart as indicators of the identical type generally return similar trading signals. As a replacement for, choose only one indicator out of every group (momentum, trend-following, and volatility) and mix their indications to verify a situation and trade supported it. An efficient mixture of indicators might be the moving be around, the RSI indicator, and, therefore, the ATR indicator, for instance.

Don't base your trading decisions totally on indicators and their signals. Trend-following indicators return a buy signal when prices start to maneuver higher, whether or not the market is trading sideways. In the same way, oscillators and momentum indicators will offer you a marketing signal when prices start to increase during an uptrend. There's no single greatest indicator, which is why you ought to combine different types of indicators and include them into a broader trading strategy.

5. PROS AND CONS OF SWING AND DAY TRADING

Swing trading is far and away one among the foremost popular ways to trade commercial markets. But like any style of strategy, there are both pros and cons when using it, and knowing those prior times may be crucial so as to choose if it's for you within the long term.

Advantages of Swing Trading

- It allows you to require the benefit of the natural ebb and flow of markets. Financial markets never go into one way continually, and by having the ability to require the benefit of that, you'll rise your returns as you, in theory, are visiting be making money once the market rises over the subsequent few days, then make some while the market pulls back, because it will definitely do sooner or later.

- By actuality in and out of the markets, you'll identify more chances. If you study any economic chart, you'll see that there's nearly always a precise long-term trend, but the market may not continuously be at a sustenance or resistance area. By being in an exceedingly and out of the market in a matter of some days (typically), you'll collect profits and identify other markets that are putting in for other trades. This enables you to spread the danger around and ties up lots less capital rather than continually having to come back up with margin for brand spanking new positions as you discover new trades. By closing your first position, you'll not deposit extra money in your account to hide the second.

- Stop losses are typically smaller than long-run trades. The stop losses on a swing trade may well be 100 pips based upon a four-hour chart, while a stop loss on a weekly chart that's based upon the trend might need to be 400 pips. This enables you to put larger sized positions rather than extremely low leveraged ones via the longer-term trends.

- You've got clear boundaries. The swing trader could be an extra technical based trader, and per se will normally have a particular area that they deem as being an indication the trade is functioning against them. Due to this, you recognize exactly when the trade isn't working and may limit the damage a nasty trade can do. Longer-term traders normally must provide a wide berth for the markets as they look forward to them to "go with the fundamentals."

Disadvantages of Swing Trading

- You will get whipsawed often, simply because the market shows support or resistance at a particular area, doesn't mean they'll be respecting it today. Also, anytime you can place a trade, you're risking money. Due to this, as a swing trader, you're risking it more often. Odds are you'll have losses from time to time, irrespective of how good you're.

- You will get to be knowledgeable in technical analysis. Whereas not necessarily a "disadvantage," it means extra work. Nearly any person can tell the trend on a chart that's going from the lower left to the upper right over time, but someone was trying to swing trade that a chart must identify entry and exit points. This is often something a technical analysis can do, but you would have to tell about it first. This takes time.

- It takes a unique mindset than long-run trading and more nerves. While it isn't necessarily scalping, the swing trader does run the danger of being "alarmed out of the markets" as pullbacks in these lesser ranges appear to be more violent than to someone observing a weekly chart. This is often a psychological issue and one that the majority of traders will eventually accommodate during their careers.

As you'll see, there are pros and cons to swing trading, a bit like the rest. To be honest, most traders do a touch of varied different styles because the markets aren't necessarily always conducive to at least one particular style of trading and sometimes can involve others. An honest trader is able to use various styles of trading so as to extend their funds. The trader must befit the markets, not the opposite way around.

Swing Trading Example:

Find a stock in the market that has been trading in the direction of the upside for the past week, and has prepared short & sharp bottoms on its daily chart. Also, determine the stock's performance since the uptrend started and note if its price refunded to the moving average thrice. If it did, and also penetrated the moving average at a median of 1.5% of its price, a good buy order may be placed. This order may be approximately 1% of the stock's price below the moving average.

When the trade has been moving, it's advisable to put a stop loss near the entry point to curb losses. And profits may be taken near the upper channel line for weak markets, and at the upper station line, for strong markets. The purpose is to take profits in line with your trading plan, but an expert trader may favor holding for ages longer till when the market doesn't visit new highs.

Advantages of Day Trading:

Trading strategy:

Day trading lets you use a range of trading strategies across all major markets. Common day trading strategies contain breakout trading, counter-trend trading, and trend-following (or mean-reversion). In breakout trading, traders try and catch the early volatility that happens instantaneously after the worth breaks a very important technical level, like chart patterns. Incomplete orders tend to bunch above and below important levels, which ends up in a flow in momentum and volatility after the worth hits those levels and triggers the undecided orders. Breakout trading also lets day traders line an incomplete order to catch a breakout once it happens, as pending orders become market orders once the worth reaches the pre-specified level. Popular technical tools employed by breakout traders contain chart patterns, like head and shoulders patterns, triangles, double tops and bottoms, triple tops and bottoms, rectangles, wedges, and flags. Additionally, breakout traders also can make the most of the volatility that happens after the worth breaks above or below a channel, trend line, or horizontal funding or resistance levels. Trend-following strategies, as their name proposes, include opening day trades within the direction of the underlying intra-day trend. Trend-following is probably the foremost popular trading strategy among day traders because it returns a lovely risk-to-reward ratio with a comparatively high success rate. To open exchange the way of the underlying trend, await the worth to finish a pullback (e.g., to a very important intraday Fibonacci level) and use candlestick patterns to form sure the underlying trend is on the point of continue.

Counter-trend trading strategies include opening trades within the other way of the underlying trend. Counter-trend trader's goal to catch market corrections that occur after a chronic and powerful uptrend or downtrend. This trading strategy is slightly riskier than breakout trading and trend-following and may be used only by knowledgeable day traders.

More Trading Opportunities:

Since day trading could be a relatively fast-paced trading style, it offers an outsized number of trading opportunities – on a daily basis. Day traders base their choices totally on intraday timeframes, like the 15-min, 30-min, 1-hour, and 4-hour ones. Those timeframes offer way more tradeable setups than the daily or weekly charts employed by swing traders and position traders, which could be a major advantage of day trading.

However, keep in mind that shorter-term timeframes usually contain more market noise, which might quickly accumulate losses if you set your stop-loss levels too tight. To avoid this, try and measure the typical volatility of the security that you are trading (by means of the ATR indicator, for instance), and place your stop losses for that reason.

An advanced amount of trading chances doesn't essentially mean more income. A trader should follow your trading plan and only place those trades that are completely in-line with your strategy. Risk management also plays a very important role in day trading success, so confirm to risk a little percentage of your trading account on any single trade.

Higher Trading Costs:

Even though day trading the market, you'll have greater trading costs than once swing or position trading the market. Since day trading contains opening more trades throughout the day, choose a broker that has tight spreads and low trading fees. Some brokers offer stable spreads, which might be exciting for traders who want to trade around significant news releases and retain trading costs low. News releases tend to steer to high market slippage, volatility, higher trading costs, which are a few things you wish to grasp if you're about to trade important market reports. Within the long term, those trading costs can quickly add up and reduce your profits.

Limited Profit Potential:

Assumed the shorter holding periods of trades and shorter timeframes on which day traders base their choices, day trading includes a more restricted profit potential linked to swing trading. Additionally, traders close their trades by the tip of the trading day irrespective of their profit. While this practice removes overnight risk, it also limits the probable profits of promising trade setups.

Risk of Overleveraging Your Trades:

Most markets don't change much over the day. As a result, day traders utilize more leverage to squeeze out the foremost profits and make the most of these small price actions. While leverage is often very efficient, traders who over-leverage their trades also risk larger losses.

Leverage may be a double-edged sword and will be used only per your trading plan to ensure to make a strict risk management attempt to cap your influence or risk-per-trade in such how that removes the danger of ruin (i.e., blowing your account.)

Market Noise

The shorter the timeframe, you're trading on the more market noise you've got to handle. Market noise represents unpredictable and unpredictable price behavior with none technical reasoning or news that would have led to those movements. Market noise presents a true problem for short-term traders, and therefore the only thanks to avoiding getting stopped out too early are to widen your stop-loss level. Take a glance at the previous volatility within the pair, and take a look at to line your stop-loss above or below recent support and resistance levels, giving the market sufficient space to perform.

6. OPTIONS TRADING

Financial operators have the opportunity to transfer derivative financial instruments from one subject to another. Obviously they also manage the related risks, linked to fluctuations in the prices of shares and bonds, of non-financial assets, of exchange rates of currencies, of market variability.

Derivatives have now become basic tools in the area of risk management. First used in hedging activities, now for speculative purposes (trading). In both cases, the guarantee is to purchase the asset at a fixed price, which will not change over time.

The use of derivatives under firm financial instruments in their own right and through their insertion and contractual clauses, has attracted the attention of many financial operators to know them better.

Options

What are the options.

Options are a contract in which a buyer, upon payment of a premium, acquires the right to oblige a seller to conclude a certain sale. The object of the sale, the option, is a specific underlying, underlying asset. By underlying we mean any security, index, currency, interest rate, commodity or investment fund that is the basis of the option. The prize is the sum of money paid to sign the contract. The right to buy or sell is the possibility, when signing the contract, to claim the right to buy or sell on the underlying asset. The exercise price, or strike price, is the agreed price for the exchange, upon signing the contract, by which date the subscriber will be able to exercise the right. The option is a type of derivative financial instrument precisely because its value derives from that of the underlying asset. The object behind the contract is another asset that options evaluate through different parameters

What are the options for?

The options are used to guarantee the right to purchase an asset. You subscribe to an option to avoid paying a higher amount than the agreed one. In this case we talk about options for hedging or selling purposes.

For example, if a company that plans to buy large quantities of wheat and fears a price increase, it will take out an option. This ensures the right to purchase wheat at a set price and within a future date.

If a person has an interest in making a profit on the basis of expectations of a rise or a fall in the price of the underlying, it is referred to as speculative options. For example, an investor expects X shares to rise above $ 10, with today's quote stuck at $ 5. He will underwrite an option which will give him the right to purchase a certain number of X shares for $ 6. If the expectations are fulfilled and the price will rise to $ 10, the investor will be able, by the established date, to be able to buy the X shares at a price significantly lower than their market value. In this case he made a potential profit of over 60%.

Types of options

There are two different types of options. The call options that give the right to purchase the underlying asset. They are comparable to a long position and provide for an expectation of a price increase. Put options that give the right to sell the underlying asset. They are similar to a short position and provide for an expectation of a drop in the price.

Call options are contracts entered into between two contractors. The seller, upon payment of a premium, gives the buyer the option to purchase an asset at the strike price. If this exercise is carried out only at maturity, we speak of European call options.

If exercise is allowed at all times, we are talking about American call options. A call option is convenient when it allows you to buy a certain asset at a price lower than its market price.

Some special conditions of options can be distinguished accordingly:

call in the money option. The market price is higher than the strike price. In the case of a market price much higher than the exercise price, this is called the call deep in the money option;

call at the money option. the market price is equal to the exercise price;

call out of the money option. the market price is lower than the strike price.

call option deep out of the money. The market price is much lower than the strike price.

Purchase and sale of options

With the purchase or sale of a call option, it is possible to achieve relative gains or losses, including the option premium paid by the buyer.

The exercise of a call in the money option is always convenient, but the overall result of the operation is not necessarily positive. The difference between market price and exercise price may not offset the premium paid at the beginning of the contract.

Therefore, the break-even point for the buyer of a call consists of a market price of the underlying asset equal to the exercise price increased by the premium. which expresses the option price. We can therefore conclude that the call buyer could record a maximum loss equal to the premium paid. If market conditions do not make it convenient to exercise the option, there are no other obligations. The only outlay is the prize.

On the other hand, the call buyer could record a potentially unlimited maximum profit, because it is not possible to know the future market value of the underlying.

Thus, the difference between market price and strike price earned by the buyer could be unlimited. The purchaser of an option is required to pay a premium and is then free to exercise the right to buy or sell.

On the other hand, the call seller could record a maximum gain equal to the premium paid, which is acquired even if market conditions are inconvenient. Conversely, the call seller could record a potentially unlimited maximum loss. The same applies to the buyer, it is not possible to know the future market value of the underlying. The seller may be forced to sell the underlying at a much lower price than the market price.

Option families

Beyond the call and put options, there are two large families of options: American and European options. To trade with call and put options you need to know the differences between European and American options. Apart from some peculiar characteristics, what really interests those who intend to trade is the expiry date.

The American options allow the exercise of the right to buy or sell, within the expiration date and if the option is call or put.

While the European options allow you to exercise the right to buy or sell exactly on the expiry date. If the deadline is 30 days, the right is exercisable once the 30 days have elapsed.

American-style options are preferred over European-style options due to the flexibility of the expiration date and for a speculative objective. European options are inflexible and not particularly suitable for trading.

The American options, on the other hand, are a very flexible tool and offer the possibility of obtaining greater profits. The option can be sold as soon as a profit is evident, or in an advantageous situation. Obviously, living in Europe does not affect the possibility of negotiating American options and vice versa.

Payoff structure

Here is an example of the payoff for a call and put options. A graph describes the profit obtainable in both cases, It starts with the call option

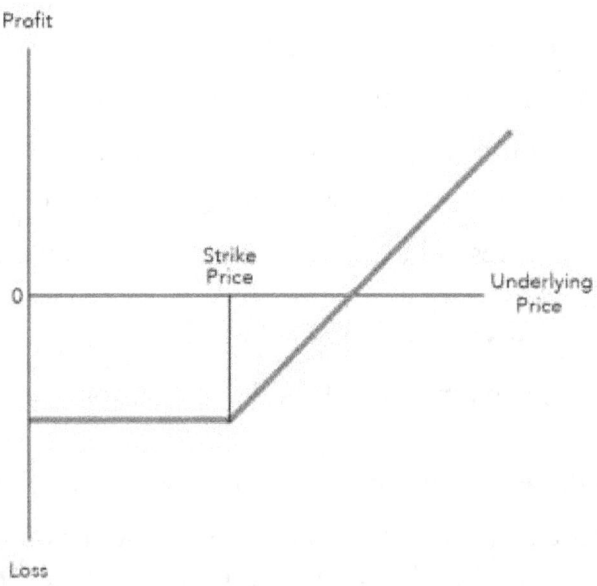

On the vertical axis there is the profit which grows as the price of the underlying increases, on the horizontal axis.

The strike price, fixed and highlighted in the figure, represents the reference point for the calculation of our profit.

Given a loss-making start, due to the payment of the premium, the profits will be greater the higher the price of the underlying than the strike price.

The call option allows you to purchase the underlying at a given price, therefore the profit will grow as the gain on the purchase price increases.

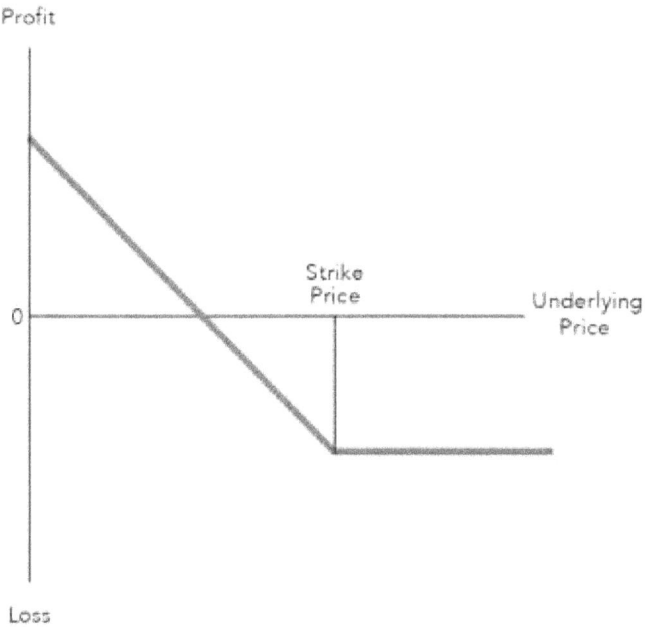

Similarly, we see the payoff for a put option:

The gain for those who buy a put option is limited. Net of the premium paid, in fact, the profit will be greater the lower the price of the underlying than the strike price.

Strike price / current price ratio

The prospects for falling prices are limited by zeroing the price, which therefore creates a limited top payoff.

The following options-related expressions derive from the strike price to the current price of the underlying, which can be:

☐ at the money, if the strike price and the value of the underlying are equal;

☐ in the money, if the strike price is lower / greater than the value of the underlying in the event of a put/call;

☐ out of the money, if the strike price is less than the value of the underlying in the event of a call / put.

In practice it is a question of defining the goodness of an option at a specific time when, if it generates profit, it will be in the money, vice versa it will be out of the money. All based on its payoff structure

Based on the relationship between the strike price and the price of the underlying, we distinguish three types of "moneyness" of an option:

☐ out of the money, if the price of the underlying asset equals its strike price

☐ at the money, if the strike level has not yet been reached,

☐ in the money, if the strike price has been exceeded,

All of this applies to both call and put options.

At the money (ATM) is a term used to indicate options whose strike price is identical to that of the underlying market. Being easily profitable, at the money options are very popular with traders.

Consequently, an at the money option has no intrinsic value and, if exercised, would generate a loss due to the premium paid. In any case, ATM is the point where an option acquires an intrinsic value.

Suppose that a trader wants to buy a call option, whose strike price equals $ 12. When the market price is identical to the strike price, the option is at the money. If the option exceeds this price level, it will be in the money. If, on the other hand, it falls below, it will be out of the money and cannot be exercised.

Now suppose that a trader decides to buy a put option whose strike price is $ 12. The option will be at the money when the market price reaches a price of $ 12. However, it will be in the money if the price of the underlying asset falls below this threshold and out of the money if it exceeds it.

Advantages and costs

The main advantage offered by the options is that versatility does not oblige, but offers an opportunity. The option allows the subscriber to allow the expiration date to run without exercising his right, even where this could have caused him a lose.

The second advantage is given by the earnings prospects. In the event of favorable situations, expectations may be far greater than the costs incurred.

Regardless of the outcome of your expectations, the options have a cost that the buyer must bear, the premium.

The premium of an option represents a certain cost, which the subscriber will have to bear in any case, against a probable gain.

The options have their own, measurable value, which makes them negotiable within the financial markets. The value of an option depends on the exercise price, the market price of the underlying, the time remaining on the expiry date, the short-term rate of return and the dividends expected from the underlying.

The combined result of all these factors determines the value of an option which, as a financial instrument with independent life, can be not only bought but also sold.

An option, call or put, can be sold and this distorts the rules analyzed so far. The seller of an option will have an obligation, no longer the right, to sell or buy the underlying. The role of the seller is much more risky because, against a certain gain corresponding to the amount of the premium, there is the risk of accruing far greater losses.

7. SOME USEFUL TIPS ON BINARY TRADING

O nline trading is seen by many people with some skepticism. It is feared that in the end it will not allow you to make any profit. Other people, on the other hand, think it is a financial instrument, which allows them to get rich. "*In medio stat virtus*", the truth lies in the middle. You do not become very rich or risk falling into ruin. The important thing to do to succeed in trading is to follow some tips, so that the well-managed operation gives rise to real investments.

The practice of trading, in general, requires a lot of prudence, if you then manage trading operations related to binary options, you must be particularly cautious and be very familiar. Profitable investments require time and a lot of competence.

Binary options are real financial instruments and represent a form of investment. As with other types of trading, in order to manage binary options, a thorough "technical analysis" and "fundamental analysis" is required.

When you are a beginner, it is convenient to avoid crazy investments. Usually, it is advised not to commit more than 5% of your budget for each operation, to pay attention to the fluctuations present on the graphs and to be able to interpret the macroeconomic data.

Each professional broker will let you know the percentages of loss and winnings that you can find. Certainly it is possible to obtain profits, provided that we are able to interpret specific factors and correctly choose the types of binary options.

The good profits with binary options trading come at the moment in which a lot of experience is gained, both theoretical and practical. The competence of the subject is the most appropriate way to be able to invest your money in the right way and you avoid losing your savings.

The theoretical experience is acquired by following specific online courses or by studying the e-books offered by the platforms of binary options brokers. Or if you want to avoid signing up with a broker, you have to study the books on trading. Given that it is your money that will be invested on the financial markets, the study will be well placed. It is the right time to devote your attention to deepening a topic that could give you a lot of satisfaction.

As for practical training, however, all you have to do is learn to trade through the demo platforms made available by the broker that allow you to perfect your skills. This is an excellent solution even for all those inexperienced and beginners who still don't know anything about the world of trading. Obviously, it is advisable to rely on a broker, who will offer you the opportunity to acquire the greatest number of skills, more easily, to start earning the first money.

The strategies for binary options

For a beginner in the binary options industry, there are numerous strategies to follow in order to make gains from trading. We believe that 5 strategies are the simplest to apply and the best performing, which can be easily learned and put into practice.

The strategies below, explained in detail, allow you to better understand how to invest in binary options. They represent the way to obtain immediate gains and avoid the losses that generally suffer when you are a beginner.

Moving average beams

It is a simple and profitable strategy to be able to make profits with binary trading, investing in weekly and monthly deadlines. The signs are simple to interpret, you just need to build the indicator, the steps are all explained in detail.

Supports and resistors + RSI

It is an excellent strategy for obtaining both medium and long term earnings. The indicators are simple to analyze and the signals easy to interpret. You can use the strategies to get immediate gains even in 60 seconds binary options.

Bollinger Bands + RSI

It is a trading strategy that is based on areas in which the value of an asset has reached a maximum peak of purchases or sales. In these phases there is a statistical reversal, therefore, you have the possibility to make profitable investments in hourly and weekly binary options and in short-term binary options, such as binary options 60 and 120 seconds. Bollinger Bands® are composed of three lines. One of the more common calculations uses a 20-day simple moving average (SMA) for the middle band. The upper band is calculated by taking the middle band and adding twice the daily standard deviation to that amount. The lower band is calculated by taking the middle band minus two times the daily standard deviation.

MACD + simple moving average

Both indicators warn us of a change in trend, a good time to invest in binary options. The most suitable deadlines range from hourly to daily ones. You can also use the weekly binary options strategy. We do not recommend frequent use for shorter deadlines, such as 30 and 60 seconds.

Trend line

Trend lines help us to outline a given price movement, when a trend line fails we have, statistically, a reversal. The strategy is very simple and allows you to get great results in a short time. It is suitable for deadlines ranging from hourly to monthly.

What binary options strategies are based on

A good strategy suggests very valid actions to be taken in relation to the market trend itself.

There are strategies that start from analyzing the facts. For example, if we want to trade binary options on oil, let's start from the geopolitical situation in the Middle East and the situation of the world economy.

The price of oil rises when there are wars in the Middle East and when the economy is better, it falls otherwise. More generally, these types of strategies called "fundamental analysis" are based on the facts of the economy, politics, meteorology. It is much easier than you think you can identify this type of correlation, also because many of these are of the classic type and well known. On the other hand, it is very difficult to predict extraordinary events, as is the case with the COVID 19 pandemic.

However, let's go back to the example of oil, to the correlation between the official discount rate, publicly set by the Central Banks, and the value of the relative currency on the Forex market. They are known correlations that depend on particular events. It is clear that these types of fundamental analysis strategies work well as long as you have an updated and constant flow of news.

Another analysis strategy is the mathematical one to determine the purchase price of the right binary option. To understand how these technical analysis systems work, it is necessary to understand that each graph corresponds to a graph.

We can think of representing the price of an asset as a function of time. Example, we mark the price of oil on a graph, moment by moment, depending on the progress of time. Visually we can immediately see if the price is going up or down, it's intuitive.

Well, at this point we move on to identify particular figures that allow us to identify what are reliable forecasts on the price trend of an asset.

In a simplified way, if we see that the graph rises sharply, then it is normal to predict that it will continue to rise even in the next 60 seconds and therefore

We can intervene immediately with a top down option of the GET type with a deadline of 60 seconds.

Binary options and strategy

A good binary options strategy must indicate which is the right direction of the market and the type of option to choose. A first fundamental difference lies in the deadline. If the market has a marked trend it is defined, it is better to choose to operate with short maturities, for example with binary options with a maturity of 60 seconds.

If the market has a less marked trend, it is better to choose a longer maturity. If the market is fluctuating, without presenting a precise trend, it is the case in which it is better to completely refrain from trading.

The situation is different with regard to money management strategies. These are strategies that indicate to the user how much to deposit, how much to withdraw, how much to use for each individual operation.

No trading strategy is successful if not associated with an appropriate money management strategy. Money management strategies can probably be considered even more important than a trading strategy. Money management strategies help to keep your capital intact, while the trading strategy aims to increase it.

CONCLUSION

Swing trading is extremely popular because it is administrated on higher time-frame charts allowing a trader to trade the markets, hold down employment, study, or do other things with their time. It may also be accustomed to capture the big intraday moves for the traders who are looking to trade within the sessions and don't want to carry trades overnight or for extended periods of time. This is only one trading strategy of the many traders who can have their own toolbox. Before deciding if it's for you, confirm your test and excellent it on a demo trading account.

A trader should be disciplined and rigorous to start out day trading. A typical day trader problem is that they act and deviate from their strategy. Sometimes you can pass before you realize you're not strictly following your initial strategy. This will trouble the victory rate of the strategy and breaks the odds. An honest thanks to tackling discipline issues is to jot down the precise rules of your strategy and stick the note to your monitor so it'll always be ahead of you during trading sessions. This way, you'll continually be reminded to follow your strategy rules. In each of the above trades, we've carefully calculated the end result. You ought to do so, too, to be conversant in what exactly can happen to you in every trade. When you get extra established, it gets easier, and a few progressive day trading apps also will calculate everything for you spontaneously. Although being different to day trading, reviews and results propose swing trading could also be a nifty system for beginners to start out with. This can be due to the intraday that changes dozens of securities can be proven too hectic. Whereas swing traders will see their earnings within a pair of days, keeping motivation levels high. At the identical time vs. long-term trading, swing trading is brief enough to stop interruption.

Online trading is one of the most searched words on Google by those who plan to start making money from the financial markets. The doubts are various. There is the hope of earning easy money and solving all economic problems in a short time and there is also the fear of losing everything due to some scam.

These doubts and misconceptions arise from the fact that most people who dream of trading do not really know what it is.

For many it is only a vague hope of earning, something that generates easy money that they have heard about from some relative or friend. Online trading, of course, can be an extremely profitable activity as long as you have a basic preparation and, above all, to use serious platforms,

Those who start trading binary options for the first time may find themselves displaced by the need to use strategies to earn. The basic idea is that a trading strategy is something extremely complex and elaborate. Nothing could be more false. Strategies can be complex but they can also be simple. Never use complex strategies if you are at the beginning of a trader's career. We strongly recommend that you do only the things you can understand.

An alternative solution, perfect for those who really don't know anything about finance, is constituted by trading signals. Thanks to these signals it is possible to copy, in an absolutely automatic way, the operations made by expert traders. In this way it is possible to immediately get some profits even if it is evident that everything depends on the initial choice that is made.

OPTIONS TRADING

FOR BEGINNERS

Trade for a living and earn extra passive income.
Invest from home, learn how to swing trade
stocks. Tips on risk management. Get financial
freedom with a positive ROI in 7 days

MARK BROKER

INTRODUCTION

Out of many misconceptions, one that surrounds many markets is options are risky. Well, if you ask an options trader, he won't agree to this. The reason is if options trading were risky, it would have been an obsolete concept in the market. Why are more and more traders and investors jumping into this business?

There is just fear that makes people think that options are not profitable. All you need to do is grab all the concepts carefully and apply them when needed. Moreover, make sure you pick the right strategy and at the right time.

"Investing should be more like watching paint dry or watching grass grow. If you want excitement, take $800 and go to Las Vegas." - Paul Samuelson

Have some patience since investment is no joke! According to a ballpark estimate, a beginner needs at least one to two years to become a highly successful trader.

You can rely on this beginners' guide book on options trading that contains all the basic concepts, tips, techniques, solutions related to options trading. Read the theory carefully and then implement the concepts given in it one by one. Here is an authentic mantra to options trading:

Whenever you make a trading strategy, think it through at least three times before your final call – this is the real recipe to success!

1. OPTIONS TRADING BASICS

"Never invest in a business you cannot understand," says Warren Buffett, the famous American Investor, and we agree to him! That's why we shall start from scratch for you in this book.

In this chapter, you will learn the basics of Options Trading with examples. We suggest you take notes of the new concepts you come across in here so you could absorb more than expected.

Here is a Pro Tip: Focus on the concepts and terms given in this. This will help you grab the basics really well. So, shall we start?

What Options Trading is?

At first, options trading looks overpowering, but it is very easy to understand if you start from scratch. By that we mean if you start from concept to concept.

Basically, traders' portfolios are created with different asset categories. For instance, they may be ETFs, stocks, mutual funds, and bonds, etcetera. Options are sort of an asset category with many frills. Meaning, they can give you more benefits than ETFs and stocks.

Uses of Options

Options can make a trader powerful. It is because they can add to a trader's income, leverage, and protection. For every investor, there is an option scenario present. For instance, one can use options as a beneficial hedge against a falling stock market in order to limit the losses. They can also be utilized to make recurring earnings. Besides, options are also used for 'speculative purposes' like betting on the movement of stocks, etcetera.

With bonds and stocks, there isn't anything such as free lunch. Options are also not different. It involves risk, and investors should be well-aware of this.

Derivatives

Derivatives are considered as a 'bigger' group of securities – and options belong to them. A derivative's price is 'derived' from something else. For instance, ketchup is the derivate of tomatoes, and fries are the derivative of potatoes. Similarly, a stock option is the derivate of stocks, while options are derived from financial securities.

Some of the examples of derivate include puts, calls, mortgage-backed securities, futures, swaps, forwards, and more.

So, what you understand by options?

- Options are basically contracts. They allow buyers the rights (not obligations) to purchase or sell (in case of a call or put) a specific asset at a certain price or before specified expiry date.

• Investors use them for generating income, hedging risks, or speculating.

• They are called derivatives. The reason is options derive their value from underlying assets.

• A (stock option) contract typically has 100 shares of (an underlying) stock, but they may be written on any type of underlying asset from currencies, bonds to commodities.

Options Trading Characteristics

All Options Expire

Remember, all options expire one day. This means they 'DIE' after the expiration day. This expiry could be after two days or two years. Meaning, traders need to think about the expiry time before buying an option.

Stocks can be held for life, on the other hand.

All Options Have a Strike Price

There is a 'strike price' for every option. This is the prince in which an option can be converted into 'shares of stock.' For instance, if there is a strike price set for an option at $109. You can use the option to buy/sell shares of stock at this strike price.

Option Contract Multiplier

Let us suppose there is a share of stock with a price of $105. It can be purchased at $105. When an option is $6.00, It CANNOT be purchased at $6.00. you would rather need $600 to buy this.

The reason is options can be traded with 100 shares of stock. Meaning, you need to multiply an option price with 100 to attain its 'premium.'

Types of Options

Options trading has immense upward potential with limited risk. There are two main types of Options.

- Call Options

Call option price shows an upward movement when the stock price increases, and it starts to go down when the stock price goes down. Meaning, you can say that it is directly proportional to stock prices.

Call Option Price moves with the Stock price!

One can share 100 shares of stock with the strike price of a Call Option. Let us suppose that there is a rental apartment, and its price is $200,000. You want to purchase this apartment, thinking that its value will be doubled after some time. However, you do not want to pay the full price of this apartment.

What to do?

You can purchase a 'Call Option' for this apartment. This option will allow you to make this purchase (of amount

$200,000) in 24 months. But this process will involve a contract, and you will have to pay for that contract.

This financial contract is known as 'Option.'

So, the strike price of this option will be $200,000 with the expiration date of 24 months. The advantage of this is if the apartment price rises during this period, it won't affect you (you will not have to pay extra on that).

Now, let us imagine that the opposite happens. The price of the apartment does not increase in value. Rather it decreases after 24 months to $150,000.

In this case, you are not forced to buy the apartment because you have the option not to buy it. With the decreased price of $150,000 in mind, you will not opt to purchase it at the strike price of $200,000.

Since you paid for the contract at a minimal price (the contract), you only lose that. Now compare this loss with the option to buy the house by paying the full price at once. You would have lost $200,000 or (at least $50,000), wouldn't you?

What is Call? What is Put?

A call option allows an investor the right to purchase stock, while the put option allows him to sell it. Here is an example of the Call option. A person may be interested in purchasing a new apartment in a new building under construction near his locality.

However, he would only want to pay for it once the construction work is complete.

That person can take advantage of his purchase option. Through option, he can purchase it from the owner in the next four years at (let us say) $400,000 as a down payment. This cost will be called "premium."

Here is a put example. Suppose you buy a home, and with that, you also purchase a homeowner's insurance policy. This policy helps to protect your property against damage. You have to pay a premium for this for a fixed period of time. This premium is highly valuable, and it helps to protect the insurance holder in case of a home accident.

Suppose, instead of an apartment, your asset was index investment or stock. So, if a trader wants to buy insurance on his S & P 500 Index, he can buy put options.

Suppose again that you foresee bear market in the future, and you do not want to lose more than 10 or 11 percent in that Index. If the Index trades at $2800 (for instance), you can buy a put option, which will make you eligible to sell the Index at $2550 at any point before the expiration date.

This will help reduce your loss. Even if the market drops at zero, your loss would not be more than 10 percent, in case you hold the put option.

Buying and Selling

Options allow you to do four things:

- Sell Calls
- Sell Puts
- Buy Calls
- Buy Put

Keep these four scenarios in mind because this is important when you enter the trading business. Purchasing stock offers a long position for investors. But buying a call option can extend your position (it can make it even longer). Short selling offers a shorter position. In an underlying stock, selling an uncovered call also gives a short position.

Similarly, buying puts also makes a short position for you in the underlying stocks. While selling naked puts offers you a longer position.

Remember that buyers of options are known as holders, and sellers of options are known as option 'Writers.'

1. There is no obligation on call and put holders to buy or sell. They have their rights. The only risk for them is to spend money on buying premium.

2. However, it is important to call and put writers to buy and sell in case their option expires. This means they can make more, but they also have a higher risk level than holders.

2. WHY TRADE WITH OPTIONS

Options trading first started in 1973. They can give a lot of benefits to individual traders, though they have a reputation for being risky. Well, you must be thinking, what are those benefits, aren't you? Here is the answer to this.

The Benefits of Options Trading

Although options have been around for quite a time now, most investors still 'fear' using them. The reason is less information and incorrect use. Meaning, if you have good knowledge of all the basics of options (like we are providing here), you are more likely to succeed as an investor.

Individual investors should be aware of the correct usage and benefits of options before blindly following the rumors that options are 'risky.'

Options have Low Risk

Some situations call for high risk for buying options than having equities. However, there are also scenarios when using options trading becomes the best strategy. This also depends on how properly you use them. Options need low financial commitment than equities. Moreover, they are impervious, which promises less risk.

Another quality of options is compared with stocks; options are safer. They are protected by stock-loss order. This order helps to halt losses under a predetermined price indicated by the trader. However, the nature of the order also matters a lot.

Let us suppose a trader purchases a stock investing $50. He does not want to lose more than 10 percent; he places a $45 stop order. It becomes a market order when the stock trades below this price. This order can work during the daytime, not during night time.

For instance, stocks close at $51, but the next day, you hear bad news about stocks like the company owner lies about earnings or there is embezzlement noted. Stocks might open down at $20. If this happens, this price would be the first trade below the investor's stop order price. The trader would sell at this price ($20), locking in the loss.

For his protection, if the trader had bought the put, he would not have suffered from that loss. Options do not close when the market goes down and closes. This happens with stop orders. Meaning, stop orders close if the market shuts down.

Options keep the traders covered 24/7. Stop orders cannot provide insurance 24 hours. This is why options are considered as a 'dependable form of hedging.'

Options are More Cost-Effective

With greater leveraging power, options can help save you a lot of money. You can attain an option position the same as you obtain a stock position. To buy 200 shares of a stock worth $80, you have to pay $16,000, for instance. But if you want to buy double calls worth $20 (representing 100 shares contract), the total expenditure would be $4000. How?

Try this formula: 2 contracts multiply by 100 shares divided by contract x $20 price in the market. You will have an additional $12,000 for use at your discretion.

Although this is not so simple, it requires a good understanding and good strategy. You will need to pick the right call at the right time to buy for mimicking the stock position in the correct manner. This strategy is known as Stock Replacement, which is not only viable but also cost-effective and practical.

Let's suppose you want to buy Schlumberger (SLB, thinking that it might increase in value in the next few months. You think you should buy 200 shares and the company is trading at $131. So, your overlay would be $26,200.

Instead of investing such a heavy amount, you could pick options to mimic the stocks and buy a call option called, August – using only a $100 strike price for $34.

If you want to acquire a position equal to the size of 200 shares that are mentioned above, you need to purchase double contracts. Your total investment for this would be $6,800, instead of $26,200. (Here is how: double contacts x 100 shares/contract x market price of $34). You can also get interested on this or use your money for another investment.

Options Offer Higher Returns

Options trading promises higher percentage returns. Traders do not need a calculator to find this. They can invest a low amount and get a higher amount back.

Let us consider the above use case to compare the return on investment. Traders need to purchase stocks for $50 and an option for $6. Suppose options price changes by 80 percent (of the stock price). If stocks move up to $5.5, a trader will get a 10 percent return. But the option would gain 80 percent of the stock price of $4.5. A return of this kind on $6 investment amounts to 67.5 percent, which is much better than a 10 percent profit on stocks.

More Alternatives with Options

Traders can find more investing alternatives with options. They are highly flexible. There are many strategies to recreate synthetic option positions.

These positions offer investors a plethora of ways to obtain their investment goals. Besides synthetic positions, options have many other alternatives. For instance, many investors work with brokers who charge a little margin for shorting stocks. Other traders work with them (brokers) who do not wish to short stocks.

The incapability to do the downside when required limits traders and investors. However, no broker can rule against traders for buying puts in order to 'play the downside.' This is a big benefit for investors.

Options also allow traders to trade the 'third dimension' of the market. Interestingly, they can even trade-in 'no direction,' stock movements, and during volatility. Mostly, stocks do not show 'big' moves; but investors have the edge to trade in stagnation too. Thus, options can only offer multiple alternatives that can give them profit in all types of markets.

Why Options are a Better Choice?

Still, if you want to know why options are a better choice, read this out:

Hedging

The main purpose of inventing options was hedging. It helps to reduce risk. So, take options as your insurance policy. Like you insure your car and home, options can ensure your investment in case of a downfall movement.

Suppose a trader wants to buy something related to tech stocks. But he also wants to limit his loss. The trader can do these easy throughput options, which give him two benefits: minimize risk and maximize profit. Short selling can also reduce loss at the time of a downturn.

Speculation

The ability to predict the future price is speculation, as its name hints. You might think that the price of a stock would go down in a day, based on technical or fundamental analysis. He might sell the stock or sell put after the speculation.

This has got an attraction for many investors to call options because it offers leverage. A call option (out of the money) may cost only some cents of a few dollars compared to the $100 stock's full price.

How does Options Trading work?

When weighing option contracts, it is important to determine the future probabilities. Options get costlier when there is higher predictability in the future. For example, when a stock value rises, the call value also increases. This is crucial to understand the value of options.

A shorter expiry means a lower value of an option as the chances of price rise diminish as the expiry comes near. If a trader purchases an out-of-money 1-month option, while stocks do not move, it losses its value. It is because time is money when it comes to options trading. This wasting con of options is called 'time decay.'

Similarly, if a trader buys an option with a longer expiry; the chances of price movement for that option becomes brighter and brighter as there is enough time for the price to get bigger.

The price also goes up with volatility. When the market is uncertain, the odds get higher. If an asset's volatility goes up, price swings maximize the probability of substantial movements both up and downwards.

Higher price swings also up the chances of an occurring event. It means, the higher the volatility, the greater the options price. Volatility and options trading essentially linked to each other in a way.

On many exchanges, a stock option allows you to buy/sell 100 shares. This is why you should multiply your premium with 100 to get the final amount.

Check out this Example of Investment Table:

	June 1	June 21	Expiry Date
Stock Price	$67	$78	$62
Options Price	$3.15	$8.25	No Value
Contract Value	$315	$825	$0
Paper Loss/Gain	$0	$510	-$315

Most of the time, holders make profits by closing out their positions. Meaning, a holder sells their option; while a writer buys his position back for closing. Not more than 10 percent of the options are executed, and 60 percent are closed (traded out), while 30 expire without having value.

In options, fluctuations can be understood by "time value" (intrinsic and extrinsic value). Their premium is the combination of time value and its intrinsic value. Intrinsic value is the sum above the strike price.

Time value indicates the added value a trader needs to pay above the intrinsic value. This is time value or extrinsic value. Therefore, the option price in the above example can be considered as:

Time Value +	Intrinsic =	Premium
$0.25	$8.00	$8.25

In practical life, Options trade at (some level above) the intrinsic value. It is because the chances of an event's happening can never be absolutely zero – even if it is never in the cards!

Types of Options

There are two major types of options: American and European. The first type can be exercised at any time between the purchase date and expiry. Moreover, Us-based options have a higher premium. The early use feature commends this.

But European options can only be exercised on and near their expiry date. Most of the options on the exchanges belong to the second type.

There is also another type called Exotic Options that are actually a variety of payoff profile from vanilla options. Exotic options are typically meant for professional investors. Other types of options include Binary, Asian, Knock-out, Barrier, and Bermudan Options.

Options Liquidity & Expiry Time

There is another way to categorize options – by the time duration. Short term options expire with 12 months. Long term options have a greater expiry time. They are known as LEAPS or Long-term Equity Anticipation Securities. They are like regular options with typically longer time duration.

Options can also be categorized by their expiry time. Many option sets expire on Fridays, every week, every 30th or 31st of a month, and on a daily basis. There are also quarterly based expiries for ETFs and Index Options.

How to Read Options Table?

It is not possible to do options trading and lack the know-how of reading options tables. Here is how you can read the options table without difficulty.

- You will notice a term "Volume (VLM)" in the table. It indicates the total number of contracts traded in the most recent session.
- You will also hear 'Bid' and 'Ask.' A bid is the most recent price at which the traders wish to purchase an option. While an 'ask' is the most recent price at which the market wishes to sell an option.
- Implied Bid Volatility (IMPL BID VOL) refers to uncertainty in speed and direction of price in the future.
- Delta is the predication or probability. For instance, there are 30 percent chances of expiration of a 30-delta.

- Open Interest (OPTN OP) signifies the grand total of contracts for a specific option. OPTN OP reduces when the open trade closes.

- Gamma (GMM) is called the speed of an option. It can also be called the movement of delta or predication.

- Vega and Theta are two Greek values used in Options trading tables. Vega represents the amount at which an option price is likely to change. Theta represents the degree of value downward change in an option price during a passing day.

- The 'strike price' is a term used for price at which someone buys/sells underlying security if wishes to use options.

3. MAJOR OPTION TRADING CONCEPTS

Options trading is a term that is used in stock exchange the simple definition of options trading is that 'it is the contract between two parties in which the stock option buyer(holder) purchases the right but not the obligation to buy or sell shares of the underlying stock at a predetermined price from/to the option seller (writer) within a fixed period.'

Options offer alternative systems that allow the investor to take advantage of the exchange and trading underlying protections. There are different types of procedures, including different mix options, hidden resources, and different derivatives.

A question will come into your mind that why a person needs options trading at all, options trading is the most efficient method used in the stock exchange and it predates the modern stock exchange by a large margin.

So, one must not think that it is just a scam created by some group of people to manipulate minds to earn money because whenever a common person thinks to invest money in the stock exchange he or she is confused by terms like these, so let us tell you that what options trading is.

History of Option Trading

Some believe that it was the Greeks who gave the idea of option trading. Long before the modern world, humans were trying to decide the prices of different goods, and that's how different methods of trading were introduced into the world.

Let us revise from scratch here…

We will give you a simple example to understand what options trading is but for you to understand we want you to focus on the example with an empty mind, for example, you want to buy stocks for $s 4000 and you go to the broker, but the broker gives you an exciting offer that you can buy stocks for $s 4000 now, or you can give a token of 400 and reserve your write to buy it at $s 4000 after a month, And even if stock increases in value at that time. But the token amount will be non-refundable.

Now you think that it is possible that the stock will increase its price to 4020 at that time and you can even buy it after the increase in price, and since you have only paid 400 so you have the rest of the money to use elsewhere. Now you can wait easily for a month and decide by acknowledging the stock prices after a month that if you want to buy the stock or not.

Now, this is what you all an oversimplification, and this is options trading. In the world of trading, options are used as instruments, just like a musician needs a different instrument to get the perfect song; a broker needs options to make a perfect sale. And its price is mostly derived from stocks.

We assure you that if you read the article to the end, you will perfectly know what option trading is, and we will also tell you different strategies used in options trading.

Risks In Options Trading?

Most strategies that are used by options investors have limited risk but also limited profit, so options trading isn't a method that will make you rich overnight.

Options trading may not suit all types of investors, but they are among the most flexible of investment choices.

Options in investment are most likely used to reduce the risk of a drop in stock prices, but a little risk is involved in every type of investment. Returns are never guaranteed investors look for options to manage risks for ways to limit a potential loss.

Investors may choose to take options because the loss is limited to the price you pay for the token money. And in return, they gain the right to buy or sell stock at there at their desirable price, so options in trading benefit a lot to the investors.

Different Strategies Used In Option Trading

Traders often know very little about strategies used in options trading and jump to trading options, knowing the different strategies may lower the risk of potential loss in the market, and traders may also learn to limit the risk and maximize the return. So with a little effort, traders can learn how to take full advantage of the flexibility and power that stock options can provide.

Stock VS Option

One must think that why is there a need to trade in options when someone can trade simply too this thought confuses many of us so here is the answer

The options contract has an expiration date, depending on what type of options you are using. It may be in weeks, months, or even in years unlike stock, because the stock has no expiration date.

Stocks are usually defined by numbers, but on the other hand, there are no numbers in options.

Options drive their value from something else. That's why they fall into the derivative category, unlike stocks.

Stock owners have their right in the company (dividend or voting)on the other hand options have no right in the company

Some people may find it difficult to understand the method of options though they have even followed it in their other transaction, for example (car insurance or mortgages).

Option Trading Platforms

if a person wants to trade options, he or she must have a brokerage account, and for that, he or she will want to understand what they what before they sign up with a broker. Each platform is unique and has its pros and cons. So a person must learn more about the best options trading platform to determine which one may be the best suited for their needs.

If a person wants to find the best trading platform, he or she must review different brokerages and options trading platforms. A person must consider different factors like competitive pricing, high tech experience, good for a variety of trader needs and styles.

Some of the best options trading platforms for 2020 are:

TD Ameritrade: Best Overall

Tastyworks: Runner-Up

Charles Schwab: Best for Beginners

Webull: Best for No Commissions

Interactive Brokers: Best for Expert Traders

Option Practicing Method

1. Stocks are purchased, and the investor sells call options on the same stock which he has purchased. The number of stock shares you have purchased should match the number of call options you have sold.

2. After buying the stock shares, the investor buys put options to gain equal shares. Married acts as an insurance policy against short-term losses call options with a specific strike price. At the same time, you will sell similar call options at a higher strike price.

3. An investor purchases an option with cash from outside, while simultaneously works an out of the cash call choice for a similar stock.

4. The investor purchases a call option and a put choice simultaneously. The two alternatives ought to have a similar strike cost and expiry date.

5. The Investor purchases the call option out of cash and the put choice simultaneously. They have a similar termination date; however, their strike cost is extraordinary. The expense of the information strike ought to be not exactly the expense of the call strike

Strategies for option trading

Options traders use several strategies to make a profit from this business. The different ways of strategies are used to get profit, which involves using the many alternatives and combinations. The most common strategies are covered calls, iron condors, buying calls, and buying puts. Option trading provides advanced strategies.

Buying calls

Buying calls or long call strategy is used when an investor increasingly buys calls and sets an option on the exact underlying asset with fixed date and price. The investor uses this strategy when they are feeling bullish and confident in an increase in some stock price. In this type, the investor increases the risk as he can face a huge profit or loss, but it's always unknown which way the stock goes.

Buying puts

Usually, the investor uses this strategy when they are bearish on some stock; for example, the investor is confident in a particular stock and had a good understanding of stock but doesn't want to take a huge risk, so he uses short selling strategy.

The put option gets an increase in value when the price of the asset falls. As the market falls, the profit increase in short selling. The risk is not confirmed as the trades return with leverage. But on the off chance that the basic Ascent past the option prices, then the option will expire uselessly.

Covered calls

This strategy provides a small change in the price, the profit is not that big, but the risk it involves is less. The covered call buys 100 shares of stock and then sells one call option per 100 shares. Covered call strategy gives a chance of profit to the investor and also reduce the risk. The share is protected by this call when the price of the stock decreases.

Iron condors

In this strategy, the trader sales a put buys another for a low price and uses them to buy a call then sell the call at a high price after some time. If the stock price is kept somewhere between two puts or calls, then we make a profit. The loss comes with possibilities, one if the price increase suddenly and the other is if the price decrease suddenly, it is spread that causes this condition. This strategy is used by neutral traders or in a neutral place.

Several other strategies are used, which are:

• Broken butterfly
• Iron butterfly
• Jade lizard
• Bear call
• Calendar spread
• Protective put

The Worth of Option Trading

When we buy a bike or car, we want to protect them; the insurance is used for the safety of the car. So just like insurance, the option gives us safety. We invest money and buy shares now we want to protect our investment, for this we use options.

The option provides us good protection of our money. For example:

We bought the 100 shares at the rate of 150 dollars, which Worth 15000. We have invested and now have the risk of a decrease in price. We buy the option to remove risk from our shoulders, and the guy gets paid now assume the risk. We buy the put option for 500 dollars. If the stock increases with the rate of 170, we will get the profit, even buying an option of 500.

But if the stock price decreases with the rate of 130, we still are stable, the loss won't affect us as we have the contract on the option which has the same price. We can sell the shares at the same rate we bought, so in that case, by using the option trade, the chance of loss is very low. It provides a lot of ways to gain profit in trading.

Option Trading VS Stock Trading

An option trading is not stock trading. Well, both of them are trading, but they are quite different. Many people don't even know about the options trading; it's just another type of trading. Few things make the difference between the option trading and stock trading, here is these point.

• In options trading, the value is taken by someone else and had a contract with it. It does not get the values on its own. This is completely different from stock trading. Option trading belongs to the derivative category.

• In stock, the numbers are definite, but an option, the numbers are not definite.

• The options trading use the contract, which has the expiration date, the person has no meaning after the expiry date. The date can be in months or years according to the option there are using. Stock trading has no expiration dates.

• In options trading, the owner has no right in the company. They have no affair of any kind related to the company. In stock share, they had the rights to the company.

Risk in Option Trading

The risk involves in option is not as much as people think. Trading does involve risk. Its procedures work along with the risk. In option, the risk can contain only in few things.

• The options trading use many strategies with these strategies. Each has its own risk. The few options work on the spontaneous increase and decrease process. This sometimes gives a big loss to the investor.

• The option involves a lot of complexity. This trading is bot difficult to understand. The strategies its self are complex. Those who are a beginner in option do not understand it well and invest the money with the little knowledge which results in a loss.

• The other problem with the options trading is that it has the expiration date, which can cause you all you invest if the contract expires. This is one big factor in this trading.

Option Account

For option trade, you need an options account. Before you make an account, you need to fill the agreement with your broker. The broker will know your investment and your trade. He will generate the strategy according to the level of trading you want. The broker will guide you about options trading and its policies.

What Is An Option Account?

The account that is used to access the option trade is an options account. The broker gives access to the user for an options account. For all the trading, the brokerage account is used; it does the selling and buying. After giving all details, you will be able to open the account.

The broker tells the two type of account which you want to open, the real money and demo money account. After all the procedures, your account will ready for trading.

The Right Broker

Before choosing your broker, you check in on him. Always choose the one with an authentic source. The information you provide him should be protected. Always check the payment and its cost. Aim for the right option.

The Best Broker

- Schwab Brokerage ($0.65 per options contract)
- E-trade ($0.65 per options contract)
- Ally Invest ($0.5 per contract traded)
- TD Ameritrade ($0.65 fee per contract)

Best platforms

Options trading is a high-level risk. It needs to be protected from fraud. When selecting the platform, you must select the best one. There are many best platforms available in the market; there has a good reputation, such as.

• Charles Schwab, this platform is best for the beginner. If you are a beginner, you should choose this platform. This platform gives more understanding to users.

• TD Ameritrade is the best platform dor the options trading in the world. The cost is low and no account minimum requirements

• Tastyworks provide trading access to different devices. It allows PC, laptops, and mobile phones. It is one of the most high-tech platforms.

Webull platform gives no commission

Options trading is not meant for beginners who have zero ideas about the market. So if you are just starting your journey with the stock market, you may have to spend some time learning the basic concepts of options trading.

When we talk about stocks, it's all about investment and turning that investment into profit. So it requires strong knowledge and experience to make some big profits and avoid loss.

4. OPTIONS TRADING MYTHS AND MISCONCEPTIONS

There are many myths and misconceptions related to the term "Options Trading" not only in the stock market but also for the general public. Options trading is known to be risky; according to Mike Bellafiore, the Co-Founder of CMB trading, "Trading is a sport of survival, reinvention, and perseverance, even for the successful trader."

Indeed, in the stock market or business, there is no such thing as assurance; there is always a risk involved with putting your money into something. The stock market or business is always about numbers and good strategies. If your strategies and numbers are right, you are in it for the long haul; otherwise, you will end up with nothing.

The winner of U.S. Investing Championship in 1984 Martin S. Schwartz says,

"A lot of people get so enmeshed in the markets that they lose their perspective. Working longer does not necessarily equate with working smarter. In fact, sometimes it's the other way around." in a trading business, you can use your shortcomings or failures for your future benefits as well; according to Brett Steenbarger, an active trader and a Ph.D. scholar, "we will never be perfect as traders. That's what keeps us ever-learning, ever-growing. Our main challenge is to use our shortcomings as inspirations, fueling continuous improvement."

There are many myths and misconceptions about trading.

Misconception #1 Trading and Gambling are same

The first and the most common one is trading and gambling are the two sides of the same coin. In trading, a trader goes through all the present, past data, and numbers whether gambling is a game of available odds.

Trading is about technical analysis you look into the details, risks, profit, gain, and the market, whereas gambling is based on fundamental values. You put in your money in what you might think will happen. Also, gambling is an addiction, illegal, and also very toxic for your mental health and behavior.

Misconception #2 Should only invest in Call and Put Option

Options are the type of contract that allows the buyer to purchase or sell the underlying asset. To simplify it, the trader purchases a call option if he is expecting the demand of the underlying asset to rise within a certain deadline, and the trader opts for a put option if he is expecting the demand of the underlying asset to fall within a certain time period.

It is a misconception about the call and put option that it is the only profitable way of trading options, but in reality, the buying of calls and puts is highly risky in trading because you can never be sure about the demand of the underlying asset for that you need the proper analysis of the direction it is moving, its time frame and size of the move. You can analyze the size and the direction right, but if your options have expired before the move happens, then you may lose money.

Misconception #3 Option selling is more profitable

Option selling is basically giving someone the right, but not the obligation, to make you purchase 100 shares of a stock at a strike price before the expiration date. In simpler terms, they are basically paying to increase their flexibility, and you pay to decrease your flexibility. So when you are selling options, you are not only using the money in your brokerage, but you are also in debt. Option selling can be profitable if you play right by the rules, but there is also high risk involved in it.

Misconception #4 Put Option expire worthlessly

Option expiring worthless is when options expire from your trading account and cease to exist. There are a lot of misconceptions about 90 percent of the option expiring, but according to the report by The Chicago Board Options Exchange (CBOE), approximately, only 30% of the options expire worthlessly. 60% of the option positions are closed before their expiration, and 10% of the options are exercised.

Secondly, options expiring worthless, only work against the option buyers, but option writers still get their profit if the put option has expired.

Misconception #5 Option trading is a zero-sum

This is one of the oldest myths about option trading. It says that if a buyer wins, then the seller has to lose. But no, that is not true at all!

Options are given to manage the risk. They do not give you anything of value other than the choice to buy or sell assets. When you use options to hedge your risk, you are transferring your risk to someone else who is willing to hold on to it. So the options trading is not a zero-sum game.

Misconception #6 Options trading is easy

There is another misconception about options trading that people assume it is easy. According to the Charles Faulkner trader and an author he says "After years of studying traders, the best predictor of success is simply whether the person is improving with time and experience" you need years of experience, learning the market and its resources completely and strategies then you can be a successful trader.

Trading is rarely about "luck" its all about good hand-on knowledge. People do not mostly have an in-depth knowledge of the options trading or stock market. It is more than just investing the money. All the experts in trading business have years of experience and knowledge, and they even use their failures as a weapon for their future success.

Misconception #7 Trading in Tax-deferred account

There is a common misconception about using traditional or IRA accounts for the trading option because they both will ease up the tax advantage, and It could be a perfect retirement plan, but there are certain limits to it. You can only invest to a certain limit through your tax-deferred account. You cannot use the money before retirement. After five years, you are only able to withdraw the income.

5. TOP OPTIONS TRADING STRATEGIES

The options trading utilizes a few strategies for financial specialists to benefit from trading. The various methods of strategies are utilized to get profit, which includes utilizing the numerous other options and combinations.

The alternative exchanging gives advance techniques. These systems help financial specialists to increase the most extreme benefits. The top strategy is used for different levels of trading. Many popular trading strategies are used in the market. These strategies are well known in trading and have numbers of users. The following are the top option trading strategies.

Buying calls

Purchasing calls or long call methodology is utilized when a financial specialist progressively purchases calls and sets a choice on the specific hidden resource with fixed date and cost. The investor expects more leverage than just owning the stock. The financial specialist uses this procedure when they are feeling bullish and certain about increment at some stock cost. The confidence of the investor prepares them to pick this option strategy.

In this sort, the speculators increment the hazard as he can confront the gigantic benefit or loss, but it's consistently obscure what direction the stock goes. If the stock goes up, the investor will get the profit, and if the shares price decrease, then the investor will face a big loss. Even the most experienced traders face loss at some point, but that does not mean it will only give loss.

The profit in it usually covers the loss of investors. For example, If the investor wants to buy a developing house, then he will purchase the buy call option by doing this he can pay the same price according to the contract as the cost of a house is 200,000 now as when the development will be complete, the cost of the house will be increased.

Suppose the price of the house incredibly increased after 2,3 years, and now the house is worth 400,000. The investor will pay the same amount, although its price in the market is double because of the option he can pay the same amount of 200,000 as written on the contract. The only thing the investor will be worried about is the expiration date.

Buying puts

In this options trading strategy, the investor has the legal right to sell the shares at the given price. The date is also fixed at a certain time. The buying puts give more authority to the investor.

Normally, the financial specialist utilizes this strategy when they are bearish on some stock; for the model, the speculator is positive about the specific stock and had great comprehension of stock yet wouldn't like to face an immense challenge, so he utilizes short selling procedure.

The put choice gets increment in esteem when the cost of benefit falls. As the market falls, the benefit increment by short selling. The chance isn't affirmed as the trade return with leverage. But if the fundamental Ascent past the choice value, then the alternative will terminate pointlessly.

Mostly the traders are sure that the market will fall. They purchase the share to sell it at a certain time as they have the right to do so, the values of share increase when the stock moves towards the other direction. It is a simple way to gain profit.

If you want the insurance on your shares in stock, you can buy a put option. If the investor has a share of 500 dollars, and he realized the market would lose the value. They can sell there share at a reduced price of about 475 dollars. The loss is reduced in this way.

Covered call

This strategy provides a small change in the price, the profit is not that big, but the risk it involves is less. The covered call buys 100 shares of stock and then sale one call option per 100 shares. Covered call strategy gives a chance of profit to the investor and also reduce the risk.

The share is protected by this call when the price of the stock decreases. In this strategy, the seller of the call option possesses the related amount of underlying instrument. In the covered call option, you can buy stock and sell the call option on Out of money(OTM).

The term buy-write is referred to when the call been sold at the same time with the purchase of stock. We get a small amount for call sales when we pay for stock shares. We have to sell calls to generate income in it. This option needs direct investment and calls to sell.

The investor uses this option strategy when they think the price will not further increase. We have to hold a long position. The chance of profit is low as the increase in price is not expected.

Suppose, the stock was trading at $200 on May 20th, 2014; The Leg 1 Buy 100 portions of the stock for $ 200 and Leg 2: Sell the 206 strikes June 26th, 2014 Call for $7.30, Lot size – 100 offers

The sum paid to take these two positions approaches - the Stock cost paid less call premium got, for example, $. 20,000 (Stock buy) – $ 730 (Premium got) = $ 19,270

If the stock value ascends over the call strike of 206, it will be worked out, and the stock will be sold. In any case, the methodology will make a benefit since you are secured by the stock you own.

State, the stock cost at termination is $ 210.

In the event that the stock falls beneath the underlying stock price tag, your long position is at a misfortune. However, you have some pad from the call premium got by selling the call.

State, the stock falls and is at $ 190 on the lapse

Iron condors

In this strategy, the trader sales a put buys another for a low price and uses them to buy a call then sell the call at a high price after some time. If the stock price is kept somewhere between two puts or calls, then we make a profit.

The loss comes with possibilities, one if the price increase suddenly and the other is if the price decrease suddenly, it is spread that causes this condition. This strategy is used by neutral traders or in a neutral place. This is a simple options strategy.

The iron condors option does not require a big investment to start a trade; you can start the trade with a minimum amount. The investor relies on the stock to stay at some particular point. It is a small strategy that involves risk, but the investor invests in a small amount to maintain the risk.

Consider the stock is trading at the cost of $120, executing an Iron Condor trading procedure we will: Sell $100 Strike Put for $3.0 Sell $140 Strike Call for $3.0

With an expectation that the cost will stay inside these two strike costs that we booked so, we make a benefit. In any case, because of the danger of boundless misfortune, we would ensure our situations by Buy Strike Put for $90 Buy Strike $160 Call for $ 2.

Bear calls

This option works on the procedure of sale and buy. The investor sells the call option and then purchases the calls at a high strike rate. This option uses the investment of the trader to get the profit income. The procedure works on limited levels. It uses two legs. These work on a 1:1 ratio to make the net credit.

Even though this is not a Bearish Strategy, it is actualized when one is bullish. It is generally set up for a 'net credit,' and the expense of buying call choices is financed by selling an 'in the cash' call choice. For this Options Trading Strategy, one must guarantee the Call alternatives have a place with a similar expiry, the equivalent hidden resource, and the proportion is kept up.

It, for the most part, ensures the drawback of a Call sold by safeguarding it, for example, by purchasing a Call of a higher strike cost. It is fundamental, however, that you execute the system just when you are persuaded that the market would be moving essentially higher.

The investor is expecting a small decrease in the stock. They sell the calls and then purchase the calls at high strike. The option works better when the volatility is high. The expiration date is good enough to handle things. The traders don't waste the expiry date, as it is important for the trading. The investor uses the long term to execute the process.

If the market is expecting the rise in stock, then the traders sell the one strike call and then buy another at the higher strike. The investor gets the profit by the amount of cost.

If the stock is expecting a sudden rise, then they sales the call and then buy the new ones which they even buy at a high rate, but instead of loss they gain profit, and then they buy more calls.

Jade lizard

In this options trading strategy, the traders sell short calls and put, and the underlying assets should not move. The cost collect in the results is great. All the options have the same expiration date. It minimizes the risk and maximizes the reward. Trading options maximize the risk in one direction.

The jade lizards option are a sort of Options Trading Strategy which is rehearsed by Traders to pick up benefit from their exchanges

If there should arise an occurrence of Straddles and Strangles, Lizards diminish the upside hazard. They are most valuable when basic stays or floats toward the strike. High benefits are created in high IV and non-bearish situations. This neutral strategy involves short calls and short put spread. It is a slow strategy; it does not increase suddenly. It uses the call cost and puts the cost at high volatility.

Let's suppose that the investor accepts this trade is a drawback chance. In the event that ABC stock moves above £25 per share, the financial specialist would lose $£1 on the call spread, yet gains £1.10 from the premium gathered for a net addition of £0.10.

The investor benefits from the exchange, except if the cost of ABC moves underneath the strike cost of the bare put by more than the top-notch that is gathered. In this model, the stock cost would need to dip under £18.90.

Collar option

It is similar to the covered call but has extra protective puts to protect the value of security between 2 bounds. The Collar Options Trading Strategy can be built by holding portions of the hidden all the while and purchasing put-call alternatives and selling call choices against the held offers.

One can support the expected drawback in the offers by purchasing the fundamental and, at the same time, purchasing a put alternative beneath the current cost and selling a call choice over the current cost. Buy one put option than lower the limit for protection; sell the call option at the upper limit.

Both must have the same expiration date and the quantity. The call and put options are out of money. The underlying assets price expired at a strike price of the short call option. The instability is surprising when the market is unstable at the point when the cost of an alternative ascent, there is a likelihood that the cost may fall and you may miss out on the benefit.

In such a case, the advantage should be secured. The option protects the losses a lot and decreases the chances of all loss, but with all the protection, sometimes it reduces the profit.

Let us guess that stock value rises to Rs 50In this case; the trader would have understood the estimation of his stock holding rise to (100*50) = Rs 5000.

As he is the seller of the Call option, he anticipated that the cost of the fundamentals should fall. In any case, its cost has, in certainty, risen. The Call option purchaser will practice his privilege and will purchase the Call alternative at the strike cost of 48, which is lower than the cost of the fundamental that is 50. So the option seller got (48*100) = Rs 4800 by selling the Call option.

For a Put alternative purchaser, an option is in the cash if the strike cost is higher than the cost of the hidden. For this situation, as the strike cost of 43 is not exactly the CMP of the hidden, which is 50, and along these lines, the option is rendered useless for him.

Net benefit from the exchange = Rs 5000 – Rs 4800+500 - 300 = 400

Diagonal spread

The diagonal spread option strategy uses many strikes and months. It works with the combined bits of a long call spread and a short call spread. Diagonal spread moves diagonally and also the names.

The option is presented in different rows and columns. In this options trading strategy, the short terms are sold, and long terms are bought. A transient shortcoming or Strength that you think would go up or go down once more, at that point, to the advantage of it.

The system is controlled on the short-side for risk, and if the market plays smoothly, it can become open-finished on the long side.

At the point when executed for cash, it permits edge necessities to be met. The investment is at high risk when it works quickly in our way. The diagonal spread has its setup, which we have to follow.

• The equal number of options is required.

• The options must have the exact underlying security.

• The options in the diagonal spread should have the same class.

• The different expiry dates are used.

• The two different strike prices.

In the diagonal spread, the bullish long call diagonal spread purchases the option with the lower strike rate and longer expiry date then sells the short date option with high strike rates.

Butterfly

The broken wing butterfly option is a bit similar to the butterfly trading strategy, but In this trading strategy, the calls and puts are much similar to directional strategy rather than the butterfly strategy.

Its sides have a different level of risk; the risk is different on each side. Usually, the profit occurs if the underlying expires at the short strike price. The broken wing butterfly option provides more profit than the butterfly option.

Futuresmag merits the credit for begetting the "Broken Wing Butterfly," an amazing option in contrast to the Butterfly, where the objective is starting an exchange at zero expense.

It is an amazing options trading which expands on the positive attributes of a Butterfly Spread. Dissimilar to the Long Butterfly, where one needs to pay another charge, Broken Wing Butterfly Strategy is a net credit procedure, frequently rehearsed to build the likelihood of benefit.

Broken Wing Butterfly Strategy is equivalent to a Butterfly in which the sold spread is regularly more extensive spread than the bought spread. It has the similarity of long butterfly spread having the same strikes that are not much different from the short strike. It works when the option has all the puts or all the calls.

For example, the stock is trading at Rs100. You buy one 120 calls on ABC, you sell two 105 calls in ABC and purchase one 100 calls in ABC, So you get the net credit of Rs. 10.

6. TOP QUALITIES OF A SUCCESSFUL OPTIONS TRADER

'The key to trading success is emotional discipline. If intelligence were the key, there would be a lot more people making trading money' – Victor Sperandeo

To be an options trader, certain qualities are required that are not at all difficult to achieve. To develop those qualities, you have to know about the options trading.

Options Trading

In options trading, the buyer has the right, when he wants to buy (the case of a call) and when he wants to sell (the case of a put) but he is not bound to buy or sell the certain asset at a specific price, as the name 'Options' suggest. The trader is also not bound to trade in some specific time. He has the total choice of what and when he wants to trade.

Why people tend to go for options trading?

Options can provide better income than any other job. It is not much different than the stock exchange. It is just like your own business; all you have to do is predict where the market and stock rates are going. You have to take a risk, but the income will be higher than you have thought. The end results can give a shock as market rates keep on changing every minute.

Top Qualities of a Successful Options Trader

Just like in any other business, there is a huge risk of loss. Every other person cannot be a good businessman. Many people have weak patience level, they lose their heart, and on failure, they leave the business or sell at a low price without giving another try.

The one who buys that at a low price takes it to another level. Similarly, everyone cannot be a good trader. Being a successful trader demands certain qualities. If you achieve those qualities, nothing can stop you from becoming one of the most successful options traders.

1. Control on emotions

2. Record keeping

3. Finding the right strategy for you

4. Consistency

5. Learning from failures

6. News interpretation

7. Being yourself

8. Patience

9. Flexibility

10. Risk management

These are a few qualities to make you a successful trader in options trading, and a positive attitude towards these skills can make you a professional options trader. Let's dig a bit more into these qualities to polish your personality a little more.

Control on Emotions

Mixing your emotions with your business can take you towards destruction. You have to manage your social life along with the real-life without tangling them with each other. You must be able to manage the happening in real life and happenings in the business. You must have total control over your mind and hold your nerves while doing the business.

Records Management

If you keep a record of whatever you do, next time you will be able to avoid the mistake you have made previously, and you will be able to see where you have gone wrong.

This habit will provide you information on your wealth to improving your odds of success. By keeping the records, you will be able to make up your previous losses. Records will also help you keep track of profit/losses for tax purposes, if applicable.

A Good Planner

Everyone has their own strategy (like the way of doing things). Some people tend to go for short sales and make multiple sales in a day. Others hit their luck after a long time and make a large amount by a single sale.

Even if they perform a single sale in a week, they can earn more than the one who makes many sales in a day. Once you find the right strategy for yourself, you have to stick with that strategy. It is crucial which strategy you are choosing for yourself. It is because in options trading, the right strategy and technique to trade will take you to the top, and the wrong will do the opposite.

Consistency

Nothing other than small chunks can be earned without consistency. You have to give a lot to achieve a lot. In the case of options trading, you have to invest your time to achieve experience. The more experience you get, the more you learn.

Like you learn when and where to put your money; and when to draw it out. Many people get back when they see smaller earnings, not knowing that smaller steps lead towards greater steps.

Learning from Failures

Just as most businessmen lose their money, similarly, every trader also faces losses. This is just part of the game! But a successful trader doesn't give up on his loss and try to avoid loss in the future from the experience he gained from his previous loss.

Then a time comes when he has learned every possible reason leading to his loss. In the future, he can cover up his previous losses by avoiding the same mistake.

News Interpretation

The traders must be able to interpret the news. If you are good at interpreting the news, you will have the exact knowledge to predict which is the product will give profit and when. If you can predict the future, you'll be able to raise your income by investing in a certain product.

You'll also be able to predict when to buy or sell the product to maximize your profit. Some news is just the hype; you have to be able to differentiate between the real news and the hype.

Do not Follow What Others are Doing

Everyone has their thinking. But once you come to the trade business, do not rely completely on others' strategies. In order to be a successful trader, you don't have to do what everyone else is doing. You have to be limitless and be yourself. You may come out of your comfort zone, but following your own passion will be the key to success. Your willingness to take risks will benefit you in being yourself.

Patience

Being a successful options trader demands a lot of patience. You have to be able to wait until; it's the right time to perform the action. It means, if you have to put your money into something, you have to wait until you think; it is the lowest price for a certain product. Similarly, while selling, you have to be patient until it reaches the highest amount of profits.

If you are not patient while trading; a huge loss may be on your way!

Flexibility

The rates of market changes every day; you have to be able to learn the changing dimensions of the market. You have to learn about the changing trends of the market and adopt newer strategies.

You have to be well aware of the relevant news and always believe yourself as a learner. You have to accept the losses as loss in any field of work is inevitable. You have to accept wherever the market is going, whether it suits you or not.

Risk Management

In options, you are playing in millions, so there is a huge risk. You have to manage how much risk you can bear at a certain time. Being limitless does not mean you have to forget about what you are risking while putting your money. If you allot a certain capital to an investment, you may be able to avoid a higher risk of loss but, the greater the risk, the greater will be the gains or losses.

Conclusion

If you have these certain skills or qualities, one day, you will be the most successful trader of the options trading. Just be patient and have consistency in your work. The doors of success will keep opening for you. The most important thing is believing in yourself; if you take larger risks and have belief in yourself, there is nothing you cannot do.

7. HOW TO SELECT THE RIGHT OPTION FOR A MAJOR GAIN

S tarting from simple purchases to more complicated spreads like butterflies, options have a plethora of strategies. Moreover, they are available for a bigger range of currencies, stocks and commodities, futures contracts, and exchange-traded funds.

Often, there are hundreds of expiries and strike prices for each option. This poses a challenge for the novices to select the best option out of many. Here is how you can do that like a pro.

Look for the Right Option

Imagine, you already have an asset in mind that you wish to trade on, like a commodity. You picked it from stock screener through your insight and the insight of others (e.g. research). Regardless of the selection technique, after identifying your asset for trading, you need to follow these steps to achieve your goal.

- Frame your purpose of investment

- Determine your payoff

- Analyze volatility

- Recognize events

- Make a Strategy

- Launch parameters of options

These steps follow a logical process, which makes it easy to select the right option to trade on. Let us breakdown what these steps reveal.

Frame your Purpose

The base of getting into the trading business is finding the purpose of investment. Why do you want to start options trading? What is the purpose behind this? Do you want to make real money, or is it just a side-business? Ask yourself these questions. Make a notebook and write all the answers that you have.

Now you might be thinking, why so? It is because you need to be clear on this point. Using options to make real money is very different as compared to purchasing them for speculating or hedging.

This is your first step, and it will form the foundation for other steps. So, buckle up!

Trader's Payoff

In the second step, determine your risk and reward payoff. This should be dependent upon your appetite or tolerance for risk. Know your type – like if you are one of the conservative traders, using aggressive strategies for options trading might not be suitable for you. These strategies include purchasing deep out-of-money options in large quantities or writing puts etcetera.

Each strategy has a well-made risk and reward profile. You have got to keep an eye on it. And do not forget to assess your payoff at the end of the day!

Analyze Volatility

It is one of the most crucial steps in options trading. You have got to analyze implied volatility for sure. Compare it to the history of options stock volatility, plus the volatility level in the market.

This allows you to know about the thinking of other traders. Whether they expect the stocks to move fast or up in the future or not, if there is high volatility, there will be a higher premium too. In this case, options writing will be more suitable for you.

A lower rate of implied volatility means there will be lower premium – good for the purchase of options (if you think that the stocks will move more and so their value will increase as well).

Recognize Events

There are two main types of events: stock-specific and market-wide. Stock specific events include types like spin-offs, product launches, and earnings reports, etcetera. Market-wide events, on the other hand, are those that have a huge role in broad markets like economic data releases and Federal Reserve Announcements.

It is important that you know and recognizes each event type. Since they have a huge impact on implied volatility and, thus, can have a great impact on the price when it occurs. Recognizing events before they can help traders to make a bigger profit, determine the right time and the appropriate expiration date for your trade.

Make Your Strategy

The first four steps allow you to see clearly the way to your options trading business. Now you are in a good position to devise your own plan after knowing the events, implied volatility, risk, and reward pay off and your investment goal.

Suppose a conservative trader with a good portfolio wishes to earn premium within some months. He should then use the covered call "writing" technique to achieve his goal. While an aggressive investor who foresees market decline within some months should purchase puts on main stocks so on.

Launch Parameters

After the fifth step is clear on your mind, try to launch parameters. For instance, you should establish the expiration time, option delta, and strike price, etcetera. Let us say a trader wants to buy the longest expiration date call. But he also wants to pay a low premium on it. In this case, the out-of-the-money call is the most appropriate for him. But for a high delta call, focus on in-the-money option.

In short, follow the given steps to make a good profit and establish yourself as a professional options trader in the market. Determine your objective of investment, analyze your risk and reward, assess volatility, think about the happenings, make your strategy, and then tailor your options parameters.

How to make money with Options Trading

An Option trader earns money by buying or selling or by being an option writer.

With options trading, you do not only buy or own stock in a company, but you are also in a position to sell that stock in the future. If you know the right strategies, you can earn above 100,815$ through options trading. Learning the right strategies, knowledge about risks, learning the market, multiplying the profit, and building wealth will help you make more money with options trading.

Earning Money with options trading in 2020

We have enlisted some special Options Trading techniques that could help you understand and earn money better through Options Trading.

Recap

Before really getting into the business, you need to recap what options trading really is, what its terms are, and how it's done with minimum risks involved. In simple terms, options trading is buying and selling options contracts.

Options trading does not allow you to vote or receive dividends or anything else a (partial) owner of the company can do. It is just a contract between you and some other party that grants you the right to purchase (i.e., "call option") or sells (i.e., "put option") stock of a company at a certain price.

It is one of the most basic 'leveraging' tools available to investors who are looking to increase their potential profit by accepting the increase in risk that always comes attached to it.

There are some essential key terms that are normally used in Options Trading:

Stock

A stock option is a contract between the company and the stock option buyer to buy or sell 100 shares of the company at a determined amount within a certain time period.

Expiration

In options trading, there is a contract involved, and each contract has an expiration date. You can buy or sell your options before the expiration date, but once it crosses the expiration date, the contract has no value to it. In that case, only an option writer can earn.

Strike Price

A strike price is a price at which the commodity or asset is to be bought or sold when the option is exercised. For example, if the strike price is XYZ dollars for a call option, then you could exercise your contract by purchasing the identified stock at the strike price.

Premium

Options Premium is the price to be paid by the party who is purchasing the right buy/the right to sell, to the party that is selling the right to buy/the right to sell, as a premium to enter into a contract for the risk of the option being exercised if the contract is in the money, that the writer (seller) of option is bearing while entering into the option contract. It depends on the strike price, the volatility of the underlying, and expiration date.

Call and Put Option

In options trading, there is a call and Put option A call is when you buy or purchase a stock and put is when you sell a stock. You can buy or sell a stock before the expiration date.

Underlying Asset

The underlying asset is reference security (stock, bond, futures contract, etc.) on which the price of derivative security like an option is based. For example, options are derivative instruments, meaning that their prices are derived from the price of another security. More specifically, options prices are derived from the price of an underlying stock.

Option Style

An option contract is made up of two different styles; American style or European style. Options can be practiced in a particular way, and both styles allow you to practice them differently. American style options can be used any time before expiration, whereas European style options can only be used on expiration dates itself.

Contract Multiplier

The contract multiplier states the quantity of the underlying asset that needs to be delivered in the event the option is exercised. For stock options, each contract covers 100 shares.

Relative Value

Selling a commodity at a higher price than the buying price and purchasing at a lower price than the market or what you sold it as.

Making Money with Options Trading in 2020

Option traders use different strategies to evaluate the trade. A list of tools is included in the process of evaluation.

The list might include; analysis, history, statistics, stability, debt, dividends, etc.

With a little reading, a trader can easily minimize his risk of losing his investment. Here are the top 10 strategies of how to make money through options trading:

Naked Call

A naked call is an options strategy in which an investor sells (a call option) without the security of owning the underlying stock.

Covered Put

A covered option is a strategy where the stock is bought or owned, and an option is sold. The underlying stock is bought, and simultaneously writes–or sells–a call option on those same shares. The Covered Put also has a higher profit in case the stock moves down to the strike price of the short puts.

For example, an investor uses his call option (buys) on a stock that represents 100 shares of stock per call option. For every 100 shares of stock that the investor purchases, they will sell one call option against it. This strategy is referred to as a covered call because, in the event that a stock price increases rapidly, this investor's short call is covered by the long stock position.

The formula for calculating maximum profit is:

Max Profit = Premium Received - Commissions Paid

Max Profit Achieved When Price of Underlying <= Strike Price of Short Put

Making most out of options

Options are like a business; not everyone can achieve high wages or income. To be a successful businessman, you need a certain type of mindset, few skills, and a little capital. While discussing how to make money through options, we don't have to only look onto physical strategies but also mental and indirect strategies.

Indirect Strategies:

Record keeping

Keeping proper records of your progress is really helpful for a successful practical life as well as for business. In options, you can track your progress, the weaknesses, and the reasons for these weaknesses. It will help you to learn from your mistakes and avoid them in the future.

Stay aware

Technology keeps on developing every day; each day, we see new innovation. To walk with others and avoid staying behind them, you must have access to the latest news and updates about technology and stay ready for what is coming next.

Stay updated

To be a successful options trader, you have to be updated on what is going on in the stock market and how and when prices are going to change. This way you will be able to predict the prices of the market and plan your move accordingly to avoid losses

Mental strategies:

Managing the risk

It is a famous saying, "Cut your coat according to the cloth." Applying this on options, you have to agree that don't put all your money into one product. Only invest as much amount for which you can bear the risk.

Managing time

No one can force you to put or call the money in a certain product until you yourself want to do so. Look for the perfect time to do so, invest only when you know it is a perfect time. The most important thing is patience. But keep track of the expiration date.

Separate practical and business life

To make progress as an options trader, never mix up your emotions with your business. If you are going through something bad in real life and getting frustrated, mind taking a break. A fresh mind can think well than the mind busy in solving other issues. Options trading is the game of the mind, so take a break and come back when you are relaxed.

These are the few physical, mental, and indirect strategies that we have discussed above. Hope, this will take you to the heights of success and make most out of options.

8. IMPORTANT TIPS & TRICKS ABOUT OPTIONS TRADING

An option trading is a part of trading that allows you to trade your market expectations while also control the risk that you are going to participate in this trading with. Now, if you get a better a clearer idea of how to rightly perform options trading, there are no limitations to it. This means that you can trade various strategies and seek profit in all sorts of market conditions.

However, this options trading doesn't mean that you have to trade the strategies of your complex trading options to seek profit from them. Instead, you can spend your money more effectively to gain profit by simply replacing your regular trading positions with the help of options.

A Little Insight:

With the start of 2020, the options trading activity has achieved a drastic increase. Now, if we calculate the increase in the options contracts in this year up until now, an estimation of a 53% increase has been calculated – in comparison to that of the same time last year. Hence, there can certainly not be a better time to head onto the trading options activity – if you're thinking about it.

However, understanding the trading options strategies and how it can be performed properly is very important. Therefore, even if you're a pro in trading, it's important to know the major and important tips regarding options trading. Now, these strategies and tips may change according to the conditions and criteria of the market.

But to give you a consistent answer of how you can firmly perform options trading, we'll discuss some tips below that might just do the trick. So without further ado, let's go ahead and discover some such tips!

Follow a Well Defined Exit Plan

Controlling your emotions while trading options can be crucial in terms of helping you achieve great profits. This crucial step can be defined by simply having a plan to work and always sticking to it. This way, you are well aware of the outcome you desire when following that plan, and you can surely achieve it. So no matter how much your emotions force you to change your mind and forget our plan while you're on it, make sure you don't!

Now when you make a well-defined plan, you can't miss on the exit planning here too. This exit plan doesn't mean that you are supposed to minimize your loss in terms of facing the downside of options trading. But instead, having a well-defined exit plan and a downside exit plan in advance can help you get out of the trade at the right time – even if the trade is going right according to your plan.

This is very important because options trading is an activity that faces a decay in the rates when the expiration date starts coming closer.

Educate Yourself

Trading options can be a complex activity in comparison to simply buying and selling stocks. And if you don't understand this activity well, there are chances that you might not be able to get anywhere in it. However, if you keep seeking knowledge and experience in this, you'll be better aware of how you can invest here and gain profit.

Now to get started in this, you need to have a proper assessment of your investment plan. This assessment can include your individual goals, the risk constraints, the time horizon, tax constraints, and the liquidity needs you have.

Don't Double Up for Past Losses

If you are thinking of doubling on an options strategy just because you want to cover your past loss, then you're surely not going to get far with this. A simple reason for that is that options in options trading are simply derivatives, and their prices properties aren't the same as the underlying stock holds them.

Therefore, even if it sometimes makes sense to double up just so that you can catch up on the loss you faced earlier (and because you follow this in the stocks), it doesn't mean that it will also serve you with profit when you're in the options galaxy.

Hence, instead of enhancing your risk, you should simply step back and close the trade. This way, you can cut more of your losses that might further come in the same trade, and simply go for a different opportunity. As a result, instead of digging deeper into the specific options category, you will be accepting your loss and saving yourself from a bigger downfall.

Manage Your Risk

Now the most important aspect here is the risk of the options trading. So when you go for options trading, you must understand how much risk you can take. Whether you're a beginner or someone who has been in the options trading for a while, having a certain risk assessment that you can handle is very important.

Once you have that, you can look into the different methods that can help you manage your risks. Now to manage the risks, you can go for different options throughout the life of the options contract – to manage the risks. These different options include:

Closing a Trade: this mainly refers to taking an offsetting position in the trade. So if you have purchased a call option in trading options, you can simply set the call option and close the trade for managing the risk on time.

Allowing an Option to Expire

This can be possible when a contract in trading options has reached its expiration date without being worked on. Here, you can also purchase or sell a call or put, according to the contract.

Roll out an Option

This is mainly the process of managing risk by simply closing an option that is near to the expiration date, and then simultaneously investing in a similar category of trade that has a distant expiration date.

Assignment

Lastly, another strategy of managing the risks in trading options is to simply go for an assignment. This is possible when you sell an option by simply receiving or delivering the shares that lie under the stock of that option.

Finally

Now trading options are quite a familiar trading aspect for many, but most of the new traders aren't very familiar with it. However, achieving great profits and success in trading options is something anyone can achieve. Only if you educate yourself in this, gain some experience, and righty follow efficient tips and tricks (as mentioned above) – you are sure to go far in trading options.

9. IMPORTANT FAQS OF OPTIONS TRADING

W e tried to include all the basic and important frequently asked questions regarding options trading. Hope they help you understand the options trading better and if not. You can post your inquiries in the comment section.

Is there any definition of options?

Options are derivatives that are supported on the value of underlying securities such as stocks.

Options are putting down your money for the right to buy a stock at a specific price before its expiration date. There are two types of options; options buy or sell.

When an investor takes part in options, s/he is either buying or selling an options contract and is making a bet that either the underlying share will rise in price or fall in price before the expiration date.

How to gain maximum profit in options trading?

According to Allen Everhart, the best way to maximize profit in options trading is to just keep it simple. In his words, "I have come to appreciate buying deep-in-the-money/deep-in-time call options despite the disparagement this strategy gets."

Purchase a 70 delta call if you think the market is going higher - or put if you think the market is falling. You will not need to worry much about theta decay (there's a little, but not much) and you'll profit 80% of a $1 move on the stock or ETF at a much lower cost than an equivalent number of shares of stock, and there's no risk of being randomly exercised and having the stock (long or short) suddenly appear in your account the next morning!

When you have 200 short option positions on, and a dozen of them get randomly exercised overnight, you will appreciate the 'simple' approach to options trading.

What happens in a case when options contract expires?

In case if the contract reaches its expiration date and you have not yet exercised your right to options, then you will lose your right and premium. The contract becomes invalid.

The only person who will profit from this is the writer of the contract.

What is the difference between strike price and stock price?

A strike price is a price at which the owner of an option can execute the contract, whereas; a stock price is the last transaction price of at least a single share of an underlying.

What is naked call?

It's a strategy in which an investor writes a call option without having a position in the underlying stock itself. To set up a naked call, an investor simply sells a call option without owning the underlying stock. If s/he writes a naked call & the stock goes up 100 or 200%, the writer has to deliver, but it is a high-risk strategy.

What is American contract?

An American option is a version of an options contract that allows holders to exercise the option rights at any time before and including the day of expiration.

What is an European contract?

A European contract only allows you to exercise on the day of expiration.

Which one is more profitable European contract or American contract?

An American contract option allows the investor to exercise any time before the expiration date whereas, in European contract options during their "exercise period" (usually right when they expire, but no earlier).

So an American style contract is exercised more but is it more profitable?

If I exercise my American contract before its expiration date, the investor might get more profit, but he/she might lose money too. Mathematically, there is no advantage, since an investor can make the same amount of profit on exercising its right on the day of its expiration.

When should you start options trading?

You should start options trading when you have enough investment and savings too. You need the proper knowledge, data, and strategies about the market. You should be able to not only predict but also implement the strategies at the right time.

How much should you invest in options trading?

It is advisable to start your investment with 5,000$ to 15,000$. Try not investing all of your savings or income on it since there is a high-risk factor involved in trading options.

When should you exercise your options?

According to Bill Bischoff, you should exercise your options put the very last-minute.

The last-minute is when the stock has risen to the point where you are ready to unload — or just before the option expiration date, whichever comes first. At the last minute or on the date of expiration, you know that there is no going higher than this, so you can easily exercise your options, although, on the last day, the tax cost is usually higher.

Best strategy of options trading?

According to Allen Everhart, there is no such thing is the best strategy. Everyday stock or market rate is different. Even the underlying asset or companies are different from each other too. You cannot apply one strategy to all of your options. However, all options trading strategies are directional.

What is a short put and long call strategy?

A short put and a long call are direction-ally the same. The shot put and the long call makes money when the stock goes up. But short put is known to be a little riskier than the long call strategy.

The short put can be exercised if the stock does not decline, and in that case, you can keep the premium of the option.

How an option writer makes money?

An option writer makes money when the stock or premium that has been bought reaches its expiration date without being exercised. In that case, the option writer gets to keep the entire premium.

How do investors lose money in options trading?

There is no one specific reason why an investor loses his/her money. There are different cases and scenarios. But the most common mistakes people make are they do not gather enough information or their lack of knowledge. Most people assume that it is a short way to become rich or may believe in "luck" too much.

CONCLUSION

Thank you for downloading this book. The objective of writing it was to let amateurs, novices, and even pros understand the tricky and sometimes hard to digest concepts.

The language of this book is, therefore, simple, easy, and user-friendly (in a sense that anyone can grab the meaning). On top of that, we have added as many examples as we could with each new concept so that the reader does not get confused.

In the end, we would wind up from where we began from – 'learning the concepts of options trading might seem difficult – but once you grab them – they are yours!"

So, just remember, you have got to be patient, risk-tolerant, and a mindful planner when it comes to business. Have a great trade. May each of your investments give you more profit than you expected.